# THESE WERE
## ACTORS

AMERICANA

# These Were Actors

## A Story of the Chapmans and the Drakes

*By*

George D. Ford

*Illustrations by*

J. Kirk Merrick

LIBRARY PUBLISHERS · NEW YORK

To My Mother, Blanche

# Foreword

All the Chapmans I have known claimed Thomas Chapman to be their direct paternal ancestor, but all that has come down from him through five generations is an ancient and handsome piece of costume jewelry. It is history that he had been a soldier, that he was the original Beggar in *The Beggars Opera*, the Witwould in *The Way of the World* at the opening of The Covent Garden Theatre in 1732, the leading man in the first engagement of David Garrick at that theater, and the finest Touchstone of his time. He was also the leading player and manager of the Theatre Royal in Richmond when that town was in its heyday as a resort. Princess Caroline was a patron and her name has come down to one of the heroines of our story. That is all that is recorded about him; consequently, many of the incidents of his life in this book are fictional, but in keeping with the color of his time.

The factual sources of this book were largely *Some Account of the English Stage*, by John Genest; *The Wandering Patentee*, by Tait Wilkinson; *A Record of the New York Stage*, by Joseph Norton Ireland; *A History of the American Theatre*, by William Dunlap; *The Theatrical Apprenticeship and Anecdotical Recollections of Sol Smith*, by Sol Smith; *Dramatic Life As I Found It*, by N. M. Ludlow; *History of the American Stage*, by T. Allston Brown; *Annals of the New York Stage*, by C. D. Odell; *Strolling Players*, by Sybil Marion

Rosenfeld; *Troupers of the Gold Coast*, by Constance Rourke; *A History of the American Drama*, by Arthur Hobson Quinn; *The Theatre of the Golden Era in California*, by George R. MacMinn; *Memories of an Old Theatre*, by George Piper; and *A History of the Theatre in America*, by Arthur Hornblow.

Through many years of travel and browsing in book shops I have acquired for private use almost every biography and autobiography of the stage written in English and, if there were but time, many personal opinions and mistaken deductions might be traced to a faulty interpretation of these works of which the most helpful have been the *Autobiography of Joseph Jefferson*, *Impressions of America*, by Tyrone Power, and *Retrospections of America*, by John Bernard.

The history of the life of Thomas Chapman's grandson, William Chapman, Sr., down through the career of my mother, Blanche Chapman Ford, is documented in the works named above.

For their advice and assistance in finding programs and pictures I am deeply indebted to Dr. Wm. Van Lennep and Miss Mary Readon of the Shaw Collection of the Harvard Library; Miss Mary Isobel Fry of the Huntington (California) Memorial Library; Sybil Marion Rosenfeld of the British Society of Theatrical Research; Miss Mary Davenport Seymour of the Museum of the City of New York; Miss Ludie J. Kinkead of the Filson Club of Louisville; Dr. Giles E. Dawson of the Folger Shakespeare Library; Allen R. Ottley of the California State Library; James T. Abasian of the California Historical Society; and the staffs of the public libraries in New York, Baltimore, Richmond, Louisville, Lexington,

Atlanta, New Orleans, Portland, Oregon, San Francisco
and Los Angeles, and the British Museum Library, London.

In the editing and arrangement of the material I can
give sincere thanks to Mr. William K. Huff of the Philadelphia Forum, to Mr. R. K. Shipley, Mr. Lawrence
Berry and Miss Myrtle Powell.

Much first-hand information has been gained in conversation with the theater men and women of the past.
I have known seventeen artists who appeared with Edwin
Booth and four who were on the stage with Edwin
Forrest. I have talked with six individuals who were
employed at the theater the night of the Lincoln
assassination. As a boy I was introduced on the street to
Joseph Jefferson, and while visiting my cousins in Baltimore, I was introduced also on the street to John Surratt.
He appeared to be a kindly old man with a long gray
beard. My recollection is that I was merely told he was
working for the express company.

But the most interesting stories were told to me by
my mother, Blanche Chapman Ford, with whom I sat
each night for the last two years of her life, hearing her
tell of the mighty theatrical figures she had known and
the stirring times of which she was a part.

In a carved wooden box she had stored away the
mementos of the highlights of her long career. There
was a handsome knee buckle of pewter and glistening
French paste jewels worn by her earliest ancestor in the
theater, Thomas Chapman. "Worn at the Court of
George II," she said, which was probably an error, forgivable in a proud lady of ninety. Tom was a leading
comedian of the London stage at that time but it is

doubtful that he ever saw the inside of the Court. There was a handsome stage jewel that Ed Booth had taken from his costume and presented to her after the final curtain of a two weeks' engagement in Baltimore, when she substituted for the ailing Lillie Glover. There was a small gold anchor engraved with the line, *From her sisters, her cousins and her aunts,* which came on a boat of flowers given to her by the chorus of *Pinafore* on the 100th night of the operetta's first appearance in Philadelphia, where the orchestra at the opening had been led by Arthur Sullivan. There was a small flower of bird feathers pasted on a cardboard by a Mexican artist in Mexico City, where she had sung the leading opera roles with the Hess Opera Company every night for three straight weeks. There were many programs—one from San Francisco where David Belasco made his debut with the Chapman Sisters. In the forgetfulness of a long career, Dave was wont to say he was the producer of this attraction from the Far East, but Blanche always referred to him as a call boy. There was a package of mash notes and poems written to these Chapman girls in their tour through the South, and scores of small pictures of actors and actresses with whom she had played. Some were people of renown, but many of them are but names on a playbill. However, she had a good word and perhaps a story for them all.

Above all there was a notice of the only talking motion picture she had ever made, a "short" shown on a program at the Rialto Theatre, New York, where in the feature three leading artists of the day had leading parts. It was in *Variety,* the leading theatrical trade paper of the country, and was written by no less a person than

Sime, the editor. He was known as *The Sage of Broadway* and acknowledged to be one of the most astute judges of theater life in the country. The last lines of his review are worth quoting: "Grandma of the cast, presumably a legit actress of ability, showed up everyone else when speaking."

In old age hers was still a beautiful face with large, strong features, good for the stage. Visitors wondered at the perfect diction and the lovely tones of her voice, "ever soft, gentle and low, an excellent thing in woman."

So this is really her story.

GEORGE D. FORD

July 29, 1955
New York City

# Contents

# Chapter Title Sketches

*(Note: Some of these sketches were adapted from old prints—Chapter 2 from a Hogarth drawing; chapter 4 from an old print; chapter 10 from an aquatint by J. Field; and chapter 14 from a Currier & Ives lithograph.)*

# Illustrations

# Notes About the Chapmans
# and the Drakes of the Theater

THOMAS CHAPMAN was born in England about 1683. He married Nora Lynch and had two sons. One came to America and was killed in Braddock's Retreat; the other son shortly after an early marriage was lost at sea. The latter had a son, William Chapman, Sr.

WILLIAM CHAPMAN, SR. (Covent Garden Chapman) was the grandson of Thomas Chapman. He married Penelope Britt. They had four sons—William Jr., Samuel, Bernard and George—and two daughters—Teresa and Sarah.

WILLIAM B. CHAPMAN, JR. (Uncle Billy Chapman) had an illegitimate daughter, Caroline, while still living in England. He came to America, married and had two sons—Frank and Edwin.

SAMUEL V. CHAPMAN was the son of William Chapman, Sr. He married in England and had a son, Harry. In America he married Elizabeth Jefferson, aunt of Joseph Jefferson, and had a posthumous daughter.

GEORGE CHAPMAN was the son of William Chapman, Sr.

CAROLINE CHAPMAN was the daughter of William Chapman, Jr., but was thought by many to be his sister.

HARRY CHAPMAN was the son of Samuel Chapman. He married Julia Drake and had two daughters—Blanche and Ella.

BLANCHE CHAPMAN was the daughter of Harry Chapman. She married Harry Ford. They had two sons— Frank and George D. (the author of this book).

SAM DRAKE, SR., was born in England under the name of Sam Bryant; he later took his mother's maiden name of Drake. He married and had five sons—Sam Jr., Richard, Charles, James and Alexander—and two daughters—Julia and Martha.

JULIA DRAKE was the daughter of Sam Drake, Sr. She married Mr. Fosdick, poet laureate of Ohio and editor of the *Cincinnati Enquirer*. After his death she married James Dean; they had a daughter, Julia.

JULIA DEAN was the daughter of Julia Drake. She married James Hayne and had two daughters.

ALEXANDER DRAKE was the son of Sam Drake, Sr. He married Mary Frances Denny, daughter of a Revolutionary War officer. They had three sons—Richard, Alexander and Samuel, Jr.—and a daughter, Julia.

FRANCES ANN DRAKE was the wife of Alexander Drake.

JULIA DRAKE was the daughter of Alexander and Mary Frances Drake. She married Harry Chapman. They had two daughters—Blanche and Ella.

*Playbill*

## These Were Actors

STARS

Thomas Chapman

Sam Bryant Drake

Frances Ann Drake

Julia Dean

Harry Chapman

William B. Chapman, Jr.

William Chapman Sr.

Caroline Chapman

Blanche Chapman

Sam Drake Jr.

George Chapman

### FEATURED PLAYERS

Mr. John Rich

Samuel V. Chapman

Ella Chapman

Edwin Forrest

George Frederick Cooke

John Philip Kemble

Peg Woffington

Edwin Booth

John Wilkes Booth

and many others

### SCENES

Theatre in Lincoln's Inn Fields, London

Theatre, Richmond, Surrey

Federal Street Theatre, Boston

The Showboat: Ohio and Mississippi Rivers

Drake's Theatre, Louisville

Chambers Street Theatre, New York

Theatre Royal, Bath, Devonshire

Walnut Street Theatre, Philadelphia

Jenny Lind Theatre, San Francisco

Old Drury Theatre, Bowery

Ford's Theatre, Washington, D.C.

Theatre Royal, Covent Garden, London

### TIME

1705—1944

# THESE WERE
# ACTORS

*Early American candlelit footlights*

# Prologue

The first actor was a father in the days of cave dwelling. He called his little family group together and made known to them that a strange and invisible power was sure to punish them unless his orders and laws of sanitation were strictly obeyed. When the family group became a tribe and too much for the head man to handle, he appointed his brother to take over the congregation, and there was a priest.

The priest invested the strange invisible power with personalities like our own, and there were gods.

The tribe was told that these gods did wondrous things and had exciting adventures. In these stories drama was born.

The priest intoned the stories of the gods over and over. The tribe soon began to repeat the familiar and final phrases. It was found that the listeners had to have a leader. His replies began to be those of answer, and there was dialogue.

The tales of the gods were all terrible and violent; each became a tragedy. A goat was sacrificed to the god and in the rite of blood and agony the meetings became a serious business. Tragedy became known as the *Goat Song*.

As time went on there developed one god who did not fit in with the violence of his divine family. He was the god of wine. All the stories in which he took part had to be in gay and festive mood. To drink to his long life his worshipers had to gather before his altar in high spirits. No sacrifices were required; it was a bright and enjoyable event. Some would sing, some would dance, some would attempt to make themselves an object of mirth. So Comedy came to life. It was known as *Village Song*.

In the great surge of the wonderful civilization of ancient Greece, it was within a period of a hundred years from the time their gods were firmly seated that the flower of a magnificent theater bloomed, flourished, and died.

There is a peculiar similarity in the development of this wonderful era of the theater and the development of the greatest period of the English stage—the age of William Shakespeare. In both cases the theater reached its full harvest in a space of a hundred years.

Many of the greatest artists of the English stage left their country to tour the United States, performing usually in the playhouses along the Atlantic seaboard. Some of the Englishmen came to stay; two of them were William Chapman and Samuel Drake, and their families.

*Duke's Theatre in Lincoln's Inn Fields*

## Chapter 1

# Enter a Soldier

Thomas Chapman walked the streets of London looking for work. The time was the turn of the eighteenth
century and everything, indeed, was out of joint. There
were no signs reading that help was wanted. Prices for
everything seemed double what they were when he went
to war seven years ago. For rent and for sale notices
were prominent in every street, and everywhere there
might be a job opening scores of ex-soldiers were standing in line. Some of them had brought little children
along with the evident hope of influencing any prospective employer who might have a soft heart.

He was always too late, it seemed.

Badly wounded at Blenheim, and sick of a fever, he was nine months getting on his feet. The only scar that remained was an injury to the nerve of his left eye, which was not apparent. Now, three days after his return from France and his back pay still withheld, he discarded the campaign clothes he had grown to hate, outfitted himself with new habiliments from head to heel, breakfasted in a leisurely manner, and invested his last farthing in a steaming, scented bath—praise to God! Now he was broke.

At last, late in the day, a "wanted" sign caught his eye: HUMAN HAIR. His blond locks were one thing the war had not been able to dull. Today they hung down to his shoulders and glistened in the setting sun. What use? He had meant to have them cut anyway.

With the decisive step of a military man he entered the shop. The wigmaker, for such a shop it was, had spread several ropes of hair on the counter before a customer who held each strand to the light and eyed it with an expert's care.

Neither man was speaking so Chapman went directly to his business.

"Do you buy hair?" he asked the shopkeeper.

The hair dealer looked at him. "When I have finished with my customer," he replied shortly. Returning his attention to the prospective buyer he said apologetically, "I'll fetch some lighter shades from my working table if you'll kindly wait. I am certain you'll find something agreeable among them." Then he hustled into the room at the rear of his store.

The customer had paid small attention to his last

speech. He was too occupied in taking note of young Chapman.

"Young man," he said, "I think you could put to better use such a fine head of hair."

"It will grow again," said Chapman. "And at present I need money more than hair."

"In my profession," said the customer, "many men and women would—" He broke off to continue his appraisal, "You are tall, too, and have a military bearing. You walk well. I watched you standing outside the window and then coming in the door."

"I was fifteen and just out of school when I enlisted," said Chapman. "I've had seven years of it. A man learns how to carry himself after that long a time under a leader like Marlborough. But that's all past. . . . I'm too old now to become an apprentice and learn a trade; I know little beyond soldiering and have not a single relative to guide me. I must find work. Do you know of anything?"

"Ye gods!" the stranger exclaimed softly. "A voice, too! Properly placed, it could be heard in the last rows." He called to the shopkeeper. "Let it wait, Collins! I'll see you tomorrow. Come, young man. Perhaps I can use you."

Chapman was astonished at this quick turn in the day's events, but even in his excitement took stock of the appearance of his new acquaintance. He was ruddy and portly and to the inexperienced Chapman he seemed neither young nor old, nor middle-aged either, by thunder! He was scented to a great degree. The cloth of his garment was of beautiful quality, his boots of fine polished leather and his linen immaculate. His speech was unlike that of the colonel from Cambridge under whom Chapman had served. This man spoke in the manner of a London tradesman.

As the two went out into the street and walked toward Lincoln's Inn, the stranger continued, "My name is Rich. You've heard of me? I own the theater in Lincoln's Inn Fields here."

"I've heard of it, sir," said Chapman, "but the only two theaters I know are those under the Royal Patent."

"And your acquaintance with them?"

"It is but scant. I was taken to both once when I was quite a child. I remember little of either."

"Stage players of dire tragedies and just as heavy comedies!" said Rich of his opposition. "Now *my* plan of entertainment is different."

"Different? How?"

"Ah! I see you respond to novelty. That is good, my boy," approved Rich. "Novelty is what the theater needs to spark it. The plan of which I speak is an invention of mine, a thing I call 'pantomime.' I myself play a sort of harlequin and introduce all popular fairy tales—*Aladdin, Puss-in-Boots, Sinbad the Sailor, Jack and the Beanstalk, Robin Hood*—stories known by almost every child, particularly by those who can afford to pay to see them enacted."

"But, sir, are there enough children who can afford the luxury?"

"It is not only children who attend!" interrupted Mr. Rich. "Adults, for that matter, are the greatest children when it comes to fantasy and illusion. You should see them when I give *Columbine and Pierrot*. Sometimes I get hatched out of an egg; sometimes I emerge from the smoke of a cannon's mouth. We *dance* the stories. Sometimes I get ambitious and present a light comedy." Enthused, he had been speaking rapidly. Now his speech was more normal. "I have to keep some of the old standard dramas alive, too. But, as you have suggested, I lose money on them all. That's principally because I've not hit upon the real thing to knock 'em over."

Chapman was interested but wondered where he fitted into all this.

"Right now I'm taking you to the dressing room of the theater," said Rich. "There we shall hear a young blade of the town read a new work of his to my players. That's the first step, the reading. I read very slowly myself and, in any case, I haven't the learning to judge such an article as this one promises to be. What I shall do toward producing it depends to some extent on how the actors feel about the parts. If all the roles are taken with fine spirit, and even fought for, the play is good. Here's the place," he ended abruptly.

Chapman came to a standstill. "But why, sir, do you talk of this to me?"

"I like your hair. I like your carriage. I like your voice. And seven years of war must have given you feeling," said Rich. "Sometimes it happens quickly, but more usually it takes years. In any case, the thought has struck me that you might become an actor."

"That's strange," said Chapman. "My father kept a tavern on Tottenham Road but before that time he was a strolling actor. I remember him telling me that his family before him were actors at the old outdoor theater in Shoreditch."

"Strange indeed," said Rich, "most strange. But we

have been indoors now for a long time. We have candle-light—there is the place."

Little did Chapman realize that he was creating an acting tradition that would last for the next two hundred and thirty years.

"Come," said Rich, "shall we go in?"

In the rear of the building they entered a comfortable looking, oak finished room. Five men were standing along the walls and two young women shared a dilapidated divan. A sensitive looking young man was seated at one end of a table on which burned several bright candles in a candelabrum.

Directly opposite, at the other end, was a chair of broad proportions, richly covered and thickly cushioned. It was a veritable throne and Mr. Rich seated himself in it with an appropriately regal air. Imperiously, he motioned Chapman to stand beside him.

"Your pardon, Mr. Gay," he said. "I'm late, I know, but I met my friend here, a hero, just back from the wars. This is Mister. . . . What *is* your name, young man?"

"Chapman, Thomas Chapman, sir," replied the hero.

"Ah, yes, Chapman," said Rich. Then, indicating each of the company in turn as he called them by name, he said with a flourish, "Mr. Gay, our author, and the principals of the cast—Mr. Walker, Mr. Shipris, Mr. Clark, Mr. Bullock, Mr. Lacy, Mr. Spiller and, saving the sweets for last, Miss Fenton and Miss Eleton."

The niceties of a first meeting dispensed with, Rich continued, "Mind you, Mr. Gay, I need time for a decision in such matters. And then there are other exacting details. In my profession preparation is the thing. It may be six months before we get a work such as you have outlined on the boards. I rehearse a play until it is ready. Now I think we can start."

Gay took up a folio which had lain on the table, opened it and began to read. He made no attempt to over-dramatize, but read in a toneless and cultured voice, naming the character before each speech.

Rich and the actors kept a noncommittal silence, but Chapman, losing the self-consciousness he had felt at first, sensed that they were tense and absorbed. He was soon oblivious of them and caught up by what he heard. When Gay finished they applauded lightly and returned to silence.

"That will suffice," said Rich, after the slightest pause. "You may go now, children."

Still in silence, the company filed out, but once the door had closed behind them they burst into such a babel that no distinct words, only the chaotic clattering of many voices, reached Chapman's ears.

Gay had closed his folio and was standing. Chapman took closer note of his features. They were, as Thackeray was to say, "the pleasantest perhaps of all" the faces of the literary worthies of the day. Chapman liked him at once, although still awed by the ideas he had poured forth.

"I will wait upon you at my lodging tomorrow at noon," said Gay to Rich. "I do hope you can come to an early decision. We poets must live, you know."

Rich rose from his throne and bowed. Gay returned the gesture at the door, turned and left. Rich seated himself again and for some moments appeared to be in deep thought. Chapman patiently waited for the outcome of his meditation.

"It will be worrisome casting," he said at last, and

slowly. "The singing will make for difficulties. We need not only the face but the voice to fit the part. In faith," he declared, "every actor should sing and dance and fence. He should do *everything* that is of any value on the stage. Do you think you could encompass all those duties, young man?"

"I sing, sir, and play the flute," said Thomas, rising to the bait more than he realized, "and I can learn to dance; I did all right at it when I was a boy. And several times during the war I've had to fence for my life. Is there more to it than that?"

"Much more," said the manager. "Your voice must hit the back wall, even in a whisper; not only in this theater but in any in which you may be called upon to appear. Your face, especially through your eyes, must be a changeable mask of many characters and moods. You must memorize as many as twenty long parts and be able to perform them on an hour's notice throughout your acting years. Your gestures must be graceful and suitable to the meaning of your speech. And most important of all," he wagged a long finger to emphasize his point, "you must make the audience aware of you the moment you set foot on stage. You must hold them partly by tricks and partly by something I've always found difficult to define—something in the personality of the artist."

"How long does it take to learn all that?" asked Chapman.

"It takes time," said Rich, "a long time. Elements of it can be acquired through practice, but the most important traits are beyond the reach of all but a very few. There are no schools of acting—you must observe and do. Then if you have natural gifts you may come to a good end. There are many people who become popular actors, but I know of only two great actors on the English stage today. I can not tell what man will develop into an accomplished actor, but when an actor is finished and experienced, it is as plain as day to me. Let him get up on the stage and say a few lines—and I know."

With an abruptness that was characteristic of him, Rich changed the subject. "Here's a half crown, my boy. Get yourself some food and return here at half past the hour of seven. Ask for Mr. Pitt and say I sent you. But, stay a moment . . . what did you think of the play?"

"I am no judge of such things, sir," said the ex-soldier. "But such a story, such scenes! Jails and bawdy houses, and such characters—cheats, pimps, harlots! He was right to call it *The Beggar's Opera*."

"All the better, all the better," said Rich, apparently satisfied with the impression. "Novelty, my boy, novelty! That's the thing to bring 'em in." He nodded his head. "I think you've brought me luck, soldier. I've a notion this thing will make Gay rich and Rich gay."

Thomas was not entirely calm upon leaving his new-found friend. He felt strangely stirred and wanted some time to think it out in his own way. Not being exactly a drinking man, he none the less felt that his thirst demanded more than water to slake it. He dropped in at the Black Lion alehouse in Drury Lane and had a mug of their strong brew. The sense of Providence having intervened in his life persisted. Not even the inviting glances of the women of the town, who frequented the Black Lion, could make him forget Rich's words. It was, indeed, worth a trial.

He reported to the theater that evening as instructed.

Mr. Pitt did not seem at all surprised to see him. Pitt himself was a sour-looking man possessing the most eternally sad face Chapman had seen in war or peace.

Pitt led the newcomer to a seat by a long table in an immense room under the stage. On the table he threw a large bundle of clothes and a wicked-looking battle ax with the brief instruction:

"Put these on. They go right over your small outer clothes. The governor likes to have you as sizable as possible."

Chapman, inexperienced in this sort of thing, had to have Pitt help him. It seemed to the novice that he was being accoutered to portray a headsman of fearsome sight. Pitt touched up his face with chalk and burnt ashes. He then picked up the battle ax and said, "Follow me."

Up to the stage they went. Chapman noticed that the entire rear wall represented a rocky cliff with an entrance to a cave in the center.

Pitt's instructions were simple and to the point. He went through "the business," as he called it, just as though he was going to perform it himself. He had, indeed, done it for the last four years and he was glad at heart that someone else was to put on this ridiculous costume and do this thankless job.

All Tom had to do was stand guard at the mouth of the cave and when Mr. Rich, who would be dressed as Harlequin, approached the cave Chapman was to slowly place the tremendous ax across the entrance. Harlequin thus properly turned back, Tom was to stand in his original place at rigid attention, and remain there until the curtain was rung down. That was all.

Almost immediately after Mr. Pitt withdrew, the

soldier realized that the curtain was going up, and he was staring into the faces of a thousand people. This so utterly fascinated and intimidated him that at first he paid little attention to what went on behind the line of candles that marked the outer edge of the stage. But alertness soon returned to him and he waited attentively for the cue Pitt had given him.

During one of the scenes Pierrot and Columbine had moved nearer to the downstage candles, within a few feet of where Tom was stationed. He overheard the following whispered conversation:

COLUMBINE: The Earl of Hereford is out there again tonight.
PIERROT: No? And drunk as usual?
COLUMBINE: As usual. It's been the same thing for the last six months. The Earl seems to have taken a dislike to Rich, although I understand they've never met socially. He comes here just to heckle the performance. I do hope he won't come on the stage again.
PIERROT: He won't. The audience has complained. The day for that sort of thing is over.

The play went on without incident and Chapman could see that his important share of it was fast approaching. He and Rich were alone on stage. Harlequin was prancing up and down with all sorts of grimaces and gestures, when, lo and behold! a dandified nobleman stepped down from the right-hand box and strolled into the scene. He came to a stop directly in front of Rich.

There was a murmur of protest from the audience. This encouraged the pantomimist and he spoke up.

"I should think," he said, "that your lordship would

have more respect for the feelings of an artist and his audience, and for your own good name, than to intrude upon my efforts in such an unseemly manner."

The Earl of Hereford made no reply, but with his open hand struck the actor full across the face. The audience gasped, but the little manager was equal to the occasion. Without hesitation he returned the blow. At this there was a loud round of applause.

The Earl drew back a step, put his hand to his face and then whipped out his sword. He lunged at Harlequin, but the demon guarding the opening of the cave was quick to intercede. The ax whistled through the air as Tom brought it down upon the Earl's sword hand. The ax was made of soft wood and flew into a dozen pieces, but it wrenched the weapon from his lordship's grasp and sent it flying into the wings. Rich held his sides with laughter. Tom picked up the head of his weapon and resumed his *on guard* position. The Earl jumped up and down in pain, giving as comic a performance as Rich did in pantomime and the audience went into a long gale of laughter.

But the excitement was not over. Now four bedecked dandies with drawn swords climbed over the footlights and took a stand with the Earl. Immediately, out from the wings stepped the male members of the cast to surround their manager. They were armed with wicked-looking stage properties, and their strange and warlike appearance was too much for the royal intruders. They put up their swords and made their way back over the footlights into the pit. Cheers and huzzas rose from the crowded theater.

Chapman was surprised at the calmness which now

settled over the house and stage. The audience quieted down, Rich went on with his prancing, and there was Tom with the head of a great ax, but no long handle, to bar the cave entrance. He measured up to the moment, however. At the cue he raised the piece of weapon with such ferocity that the curtain came down to round after round of applause.

His theatrical debut at an end, Tom found his way back to the dressing room, got out of his costume and, with a soldier's neatness, folded it carefully, laid it on the table and placed the piece of weapon atop it. He had a feeling he might not be needing it again.

It was at this moment Pitt hurried to him. He was all smiles for once as he notified Tom that Mr. Rich wished to walk with him to his lodgings when the play was over.

As Tom stood waiting by the stage door, the departing actors all shook his hand with profound compliments, and one pretty young creature he hadn't even noticed didn't say a word but actually kissed him. Last of all came Rich, and the two men strolled through the silent town.

"My boy," said Rich, "I'm sure you saved me from great harm tonight, perhaps from death, and I'm not an ungrateful man."

"It all came without thinking, sir," Tom replied.

"It saved the play and me," said the manager. "Where are you stopping?"

"To tell the truth," said the novice, "the excitement of meeting you, along with the events at the theater, has driven all thought of lodging from my head. I have yet to find a place."

"You'll come with me," said Rich. They walked to a

place called Blumsbury and he led the way around to the rear of a large house. There he opened a small door.

"This is your room for as long as you like," he said. "It has its own entrance. No one will use it but you. The pump is in this corner of the yard and the privy over there back of the orchard. A tall candle always burns there and snuffs itself out about one o'clock. Good night, pleasant dreams, and thanks again."

Chapman looked about the very cheerful room furnished with a large easy wing chair, a handsome bed, a carpet, a pitcher, a washboard and a bucket of clear water. All this in one short December day! Surely being an actor was a beautiful, luxurious life.

*Rich parade enters Covent Garden Theatre*

## Chapter 2

# A Piece of Business

It took Tom Chapman no time at all to become proficient in the duties of a spear carrier on the stage of Mr. Rich's theater. Acting was easy enough becoming accustomed to but it was quite another matter trying to understand the house in which he lived and its master. One thing was certain: everyone in service at the house doubled in duty at the theater.

One man had charge of a room next to that of Mr. Rich. This room was set aside for twenty-four cats. Their caretaker fed the felines and cleaned the chamber each night. There was an appointed time each morning when the door leading into Mr. Rich's bedroom was opened and the little creatures ushered in. There, for an hour, he fondled the furry troupe and tried to teach them tricks. When the hour was up they were led back to their private apartment. The caretaker of the cats also took tickets at the theater.

Rich's valet and servant was the man who had charge of all props used on stage by the artists. The man who built the scenery for the plays also did the repairs on Rich's fences and outhouses. Mr. Pitt turned out to be the cook. Mr. Glover, the chamberman and candle watcher at home, was in charge of the illusions for the dances at the theater. His latest invention was the talk of the town, a row of candles with reflectors placed in front of the actors at the foot of the stage. From this they were called *footlights*.

With these and other things, Tom found Mr. Rich a strange fellow, the more so because the manager took such a strong liking to him. He always shook Chapman's hand when meeting and parting and insisted the young man walk home with him each night. There was such a flood of talk from him the entire way that Tom seldom could slip in more than a word or two of his own.

The relationship may have provided a sort of confessional for the many sins of trade committed by Mr. Rich, or it may have arisen as a relief from the worries of the theater. It also could have been that he wanted the young soldier coupled to him with loops of steel in case something like the Earl of Hereford episode should arise again. In addition to his valiant appearance and proven bravery, Tom had another quality the manager admired. He was a discreet young man and no critical word of the theater or company ever came from him. There were many willing spies about and there was little that did not come to the ear of Mr. Rich before a day was over. Chapman at first thought he was to be enrolled as a talebearer, but as time went on and no questions came from Mr. Rich, there was no need of an answer from Mr. Chapman.

Seldom was anyone except the housemaid and a man-servant permitted to enter the manager's chamber, but almost from the start he had insisted that Tom was always welcome.

Rich's room was as inexplicable as its owner. A full-length mirror with three panels resembling the fender of a fireplace fanned out behind a table laden with many odd-sized bottles and bowls. These, Chapman learned, were the lotions, creams, powders and perfumes with which Mr. Rich worked on his face and general personal appearance. This took at least an hour each morning, a period of the day which, with Mr. Rich, ran well into the early hours of the afternoon.

To one side of the mirror stood a wig rack on which hung—Tom once counted them—twenty wigs; blond, brunette, red, iron gray, gray-white, all white and several with white streaks running through solid colors. Mr. Rich wore them in rotation, without caring for the fact that nature never performed such miracles. His own growth consisted of a ring of dull brownish-gray hair encircling an almost totally bald spot. He always ad-justed his wig carefully to let a wisp of his own hair show through, just to prove he had plenty of hair if he cared to expose it. But no mortal ever saw him without his wig. When Chapman knocked he was bade to enter almost immediately, and although the wig might have been clapped on askew at that moment, it was always on nevertheless.

Within easy reach was his medicine chest filled with bottles of pills and tonics of all kinds. There was also a large roll of white cloth and a sharpened knife in case there should ever be need for an emergency surgical operation.

At hand also was his wine and liquor cabinet, the key for which he always carried on his person. The making of the nightcap was a ritual indeed. It took a full quarter hour to mix it to the proper consistency, after which Mr. Rich sipped it as comfortably as one would milk, while Chapman suffered great agonies from a burning throat.

At first Tom thought that the old man was grooming him to step into his managerial shoes, but he found out later that this strange little man was bidding a fond fare-well to the theater as a property and, having neither wife nor child, was leaving his entire fortune to a home for indigent actors and actresses. Nothing ever came of this. Like many other noted theatrical producers, the great Mr. Rich lost heavily at the last and died leaving almost nothing.

But during his early years Rich was a most productive and alert man of the theater. He was especially adept at puffing—the art of getting something talked about and arousing such interest in it that people wanted to see it in a theater.

"Never," he said to Tom, "miss a single chance to call attention to what you have. Some of us are born to be talked about, some of us achieve it and some have it

thrust upon us, but we *must* have it in the theater. Now,
I am sure you have noticed that I have various set ways
of going about this. You see this small piece of paper?"
He indicated a scrap in his hand. "It is called an order.
It is a most powerful thing. With my signature on it,
it is good for two box seats on a given date. But not
exactly for nothing, as I will shortly illustrate.

"You well know that you can not go into a store and
get a shirt of even the cheapest fabric for nothing. That
shirt can probably be sold later on. But, mark you, you
can not sell an order for two seats in a theater marked
for a *past* date. A cart full of them would not be worth
threepence at half past nine. But this order for a certain
night yet to come can work wonders. Many folks will
pay more for them than the stated price. Why? Because
they can show them to friends with the inference that
they have some secret interest in the business of the
theater. They can count themselves silent partners of
Mr. Rich of Lincoln's Inn Fields.

"But," he hastened to assure his listener, "not anyone
can get an order. I am most careful about who gets them.
By marking them for the boxes I can get the nobility, the
statesmen, the ladies and gentlemen to come; and when
that is noised about, the crowd will follow. Sometimes
the crowd is more anxious to see our ruling families than
the plays. People were trampled to death at the doors
when the King visited.

"But the most important use is this: At each inn I
station an impressive, well-spoken man to secretly talk
up—well, just what I want him to. I name the play, its
subject, its special incidents, its actors—and this man
stirs up interest in it in advance of the performance of

the play. He does all this for nothing, or at least, for this small piece of paper which costs me nothing. At times I resort to something we call a gag, some planned sensational action, some surprising feature. I have a tremendous one in mind right now. You'll soon see what it is. This one, my man, has more to do with a theater than a play."

At that time the building of the much-discussed Covent Garden Theatre had begun. The front was completed and the directors had offices on the second floor above Bow Street. Meetings were held there to discuss managerial policy. The main objective was to draw heavily on the cream of the patronage which supported the already established Drury Lane Theatre.

Mr. Rich had sent in an offer to lease the house, and in keeping with the florid phrase-heavy style of the times had signed it: *I am, with profound respect, My Lords, Your Graces' Most Obedient Humble Servant.* But while the investors, at least, knew that it took keen perception and great experience to produce an attraction that would not suffer in comparison to the structure which housed it, few "in the know" gave Rich's bid more than token consideration. Too many gentlemen of high estate, and even members of the nobility, had a fancy for this fascinating dilettante's delight. The forces of influence and prestige were at work.

One day as Tom was leaving Mr. Rich's room he saw a manservant enter, followed by three men. This was an unprecedented occurrence, that strangers be admitted to the Rich sanctum, so Tom took a good look. Four days later he saw these same three men working as surveyors in the neighborhood of the new Covent Garden Theatre.

They sighted, they waved, they measured and they called to one another in strange technical terms. They were at it an interval of every three days until, at last, they wound up their surveying right across the street from the striking new edifice on Bow Street.

Those worthies inside, who were financially involved in the Covent Garden venture and who were still deliberating over the lessee, could see these fellows from their office window. It looked threatening enough and set them thinking, for it was rumored that Mr. Rich intended giving up his theater out in the Fields and building a new home for his "Company of Comedians" in the very center of town.

This was opposition, indeed. Here was the man who had boldly produced *The Beggar's Opera*. Before that time Rich had seldom been able to fill his house without orders. But with the Gay innovation to his credit nothing could keep them away. The side boxes were invariably filled by distinguished persons. In London, with a population of 400,000, it had played to capacity for sixty-three consecutive nights and still was the talk of the town. Ladies of the court had the lyrics printed on their fans and the music was hummed throughout the country. The song, "When you censure the age . . ." was taken as an allusion to the incumbent Minister, Sir Robert Walpole. He took the mocking criticism with surprisingly good grace by joining in with the audience for a second encore, bringing huzzas for himself and thereby adding to public clamor to see the play.

It was revived at the opening of the London theater the next season, and its success spread to all the larger towns where in many instances it played thirty to forty times. In Bristol and Bath it ran for fifty performances. It was also noted that gangs of robbers multiplied wherever it was produced!

Gay's masterpiece, and Rich's startling stroke of good fortune in producing it, was a sensational departure in opera form. It was the first ballad opera, which means that instead of creating the opera around specially composed music, old ballad airs are used with new words added to fit the plot. It supplanted Italian opera in England to the extent that even Handel's scores, as well as works of other worthy contemporaries, could not stand up against it. Its extreme popularity was also attested to by the fact that even after its initial overwhelming success it was often used by both the Covent Garden and Drury Lane theaters at the same time, with no outstanding loss suffered by either house. It gained popularity by making a topical jest of politics and thievery in an age when these skills were unduly romanticized.

Rich's "surveyors" were a tremendous success. Under his management, *The Beggar's Opera* was the second production at Covent Garden. It ran for twenty nights and then was transferred again to its original home— Lincoln's Inn Fields.

The original presentation of *The Beggar's Opera* has always been a source of great interest to the Chapman family, for Thomas Chapman played the small but important title role, appearing with such talented contemporaries of his day as Hippefley, Hall, Walker, Clark and Milward. Even in 1948, one of Tom Chapman's descendants enacted the Beggar in a revival by the Drama Department at McGill University, Montreal.

Mr. Rich's activities up to the time of Covent Garden's completion were well-known to the sponsors of that expensive undertaking. They also knew that Rich had some of the leading actors and actresses under his thumb and that he controlled several of the most popular vehicles in which they would appear. Now here he was, not only buying up property in the neighborhood, but right across the street! Small wonder they decided to ignore pressure from less formidable sources and take matters into their own hands.

So Mr. Rich was sent for by the management to discuss his qualifications. He brought a large satchel with him, and entered the office with all the awe and humility that the occasion required. He sustained this pose until the satchel was opened and laid before the conferees. It was filled with ten-pound notes. Then he began to talk.

The eloquence of his speech, the persuasiveness of the satchel's contents, and the alarming implications behind the surveying all contributed to his triumph. He was given the lease.

Once the matter was settled, public and professional interest combined to make this the most publicized theater opening in history; but no one discussed it more earnestly than the staff of players at the Theatre in Lincoln's Inn Fields. Each actor speculated on what attraction would open the house and what part he would play in it. Mr. Rich remained silent, that is, with everyone except Tom Chapman. Rich called him in one night and asked him to play Witwould in *The Way of the World*.

Tom was astonished. This difficult part had originally been written for the famous Colley Cibber, who was now Poet Laureate. Cibber had been manager of the rival Drury Lane and had rejected *The Beggar's Opera* shortly before Rich accepted it.

Tom had never seen Cibber in the Witwould role but had played it himself at the fairs, since joining Rich's company, and had his own ideas of how it should be done on the new stage.

"I'll play it, governor," he said, "and I'll work hard."

"Then it's settled," said Rich. "We open December sixth in this year of our Lord, 1732. Now all that remains is to think up a gag to get started."

Tom had no doubt that the manager would outdo himself in this instance, and about four days later he was again called to the bedroom of Mr. Rich. The little man was beaming.

"I've got it!" he said. "Not one gag, but two! They will revolutionize the way to create interest."

"I am genuinely glad, sir," said Chapman. "Are you of the mind to relate them?"

"I am that!" responded the exuberant Rich. "You shall hear of them both in detail. First, think of this: We'll parade from the old house to Covent Garden. All my actors will dress in the costumes they are most noted for. Our scenery will be handled in ten vans. Of course, we haven't that much scenery, but I'll have some boxes built and borrow some crates. We'll march right through the city and have some of my men cheer and shout 'Rich Forever!' It will wake up the town. The only thing that can stop us is a hard rain. What do you think of that?"

"A parade, sir, sounds like a tremendous idea! Will the actors consent?" asked Tom.

"I have ways to make 'em," said the manager in curt dismissal of such a concern. "Now, my second gag is this: You know that pudgy young man that takes his order for every show and likes to come backstage to chat with the ladies of the cast?"

Tom nodded.

"That's Hogarth, the coming painter and engraver of the city," said Rich. "I'll get him to make a sketch of the parade. I'll have it run off—printed—and a copy hung in every inn and tavern in town. A picture like that can speak louder than any notice in the *Gazette* or fanfare by any of my lecturers. Those fellows are an unnecessary expense anyway. They're asking for more orders now; soon they'll want *money*. They think I should at least pay for their drinking. But just let me hang one of Mr. Hogarth's pictures in their stations! The innkeeper can get the order."

Mr. Rich swelled with confidence and pride.

"These two ideas of mine, my boy—the parade and the picture posted in a public place—are among the greatest gags ever thought up. They won't fail to draw a crowd."

*Covent Garden Greenroom*

*Chapter 3*

# A Bright Particular Star

Of all those who doubled in duty at the theater in the
Fields and Mr. Rich's abode, the old woman who helped
dress the ladies for the stage and took general care of
their costumes had the most important job of all. By day
she guarded the front door of the residence like a turnkey
at Newgate. It was her business to know the business of
everyone who had any doings with the master, and there
were no mistakes. She either knew the history of every
caller, or by their manner and personal appearance judged
whether or not Rich would want to see them.

Because of his hard work and Rich's approbation,

Chapman was established now as an actor. Mostly he played fops and young heirs of rich uncles, characters that were written into every play. If he had not held that prominent position he might never have met the "Dark Lady" of his life.

Late in the first season with the troupe he began to notice that a lovely young woman was being turned away from the door of the Rich home a number of times. Her persistence first caught his attention, but then he was held by her looks and manner. She had both beauty and determination. She stood up to the gaunt keeper of the gate with the lilting tongue and aggressive tone of a true daughter of the *Emerald Isle*.

Once, at a distance of perhaps half a mile from the Rich house, Tom met her coming away with tears coursing down her cheeks and sobbing quite audibly. He was a diffident man but he was also a chivalrous one, and so he stopped her.

"Mistress," he said, "I am Thomas Chapman of the theater in the Fields and live at the Rich house. I have noticed. . . ."

She broke in on him. "I have seen you on the stage and I know your house. I'm an actress from Dublin. Right now it seems very far away. I've called eighteen times in an effort to have your manager place me. There is no other work I know how to do and I have just one pound left."

There came more tears and a fresh outburst of sobs. But there was a flash in the lovely blue eyes as she went on, "If I have to go back without seeing him, I'll get even with him if I die for it."

"A creature like you should not have to worry about

living in need," said Chapman. "I'll take you home now and on the way I'll tell you of the scheme I have in mind."

The next morning Chapman happened, by design, to pass the door of the room where the ticket taker was preparing to escort the cats to their master. After checking the time of day and chatting on other equally unimportant matters, Tom bade the man farewell, and left with a slight bulge under his coat. He then went from the premises to a certain shaded spot around the corner.

In not more than half an hour the lovely colleen again appeared at the front door of the Rich abode. There was a half-grown cat draped over her shoulder and she demanded to see the manager. The old witch was as adamant as ever, but the young woman raised her voice a pitch higher with every new key the doorkeeper reached. The talk grew louder than the wailing of any two Kilkenny cats, for the old girl was also of the *Auld Sod*.

Tom Chapman came running to the door.

"I tell you it is Mr. Rich's cat and I will give it to no one but him," sang the maiden. "If he doesn't want it, I'll keep it myself and teach it more tricks than any man could. See how it puts its paws around my neck!"

Tom ran back to the apartment of Mr. Rich.

"I know my business," shouted the wardrobe mistress, "and I know my orders. If I let all the likes of you in Mr. Rich would have no time to run the theater. We'd all be out of work and living off the town in no time."

The girl's reply was a half tone higher, but before she had finished her tirade Tom was on the scene again with word that Rich would see her. He led the way down the hall.

As he grasped the doorknob to let her into the august
presence the girl patted him on the shoulder and mur-
mured, "Enter, Elizabeth."

Tom closed the door and tiptoed away.

The girl's eyes quickly became accustomed to the dim
light of the room. Far in a darkened corner sat Mr. Rich,
seemingly surrounded and covered with cats both great
and small. His visitor afterward learned that there were
really just twenty-three of them. She held as hostage the
twenty-fourth.

"My name is—" she began.

But he interrupted, "Your name is Murphy. You are
an Irish actress, which means little to me. Most likely,
you're up from the Dublin gutter, which is nothing
against your acting. I know the parts you've played and
I think I know how you've played them. Your appearance is good, however, and you've done me a favor in
returning my cat, so I'll hear you read. But, even if I
like it you may have to wait a very long time before I
can use you. Meanwhile you must give up thought of
everything else. Now, bring me my cat, please."

"Miss Murphy" found a niche for the little animal on
the shoulders of the great man.

"Stand there and give me a taste of your mettle," he
directed.

While the girl walked to where he pointed, Rich pulled
on a cord near his chair. This let down a shade at one
of the windows and bathed his head in a flood of morning
sunlight. He had a flair for the dramatic, but, truth to
tell, this action added little of distinction to his appearance and had no apparent effect on Miss Murphy.

She stood at ease in the dark corner and said, "What
would you see and hear?"

"Give me a bit of Viola, Ophelia, Desdemona and Cordelia."

Miss Murphy did as she was bid.

"Now Lady Brecken in *The Careless Husband*."

Without the slightest hesitation the girl reeled it off, even following with the parts of five other characters the manager called for. Then he seemed lost in thought while she waited.

Suddenly he said, "Let me see your legs."

Without a change of expression and as quickly as she had recited the parts, the girl lifted her skirts to above her knees.

"Your voice is heavy," said Rich, "too heavy for the parts you have read me, but it has given me an idea. Your legs, too. Since boys gave up the playing of women on the stage I've often thought of a woman playing a boy —a young spark, the fop all the plays seem to require. There's one I dearly love, Sir Harry Wildair."

"I know it already," the girl broke in. "I've practiced the walk and the business with the handkerchief, the snuff box, the purse, the sword. . . ."

"Not so fast!" said Rich. "I'm weary now and have neglected my little friends here. Please leave and next time, see me at the theater. I will see to it that you are always welcome there. We'll work on Wildair later."

The girl made a graceful curtsy and left.

Chapman was waiting for her a short distance down the street, but she passed him with a smile and one simple speech: "I'm too excited now. Thank you so much. I'll never forget this."

Tom Chapman never forgot her. Peg Woffington became the *other woman* in his life, unattainable—not desired, really, in the full sense of the term, for to have possessed her would have ruined the illusion. And Tom had a love life thoroughly satisfying and inspiring. Nora Lynch, the darling who had kissed him on the night of his professional debut, eventually became first his sweetheart and then his wife. They were devoted to each other and had two sons.

The years in London sped quickly by as he raised his family and became a leading actor. During his first season with the Rich Company in Covent Garden he played the second male lead to the rising Garrick and quite handsomely held his own. He played the English fairs and, for a while, had his own playhouse in Richmond. His life with the theater was quite complete, but he still had the need to trace the rising star of his Irish princess.

Then, at long last, he was to play the role he excelled in, Touchstone, and she would play Rosalind. Touchstone to her Rosalind!

For the most part she had played at the theaters of Rich's competitors and was seldom seen in the old haunts. Tom, coming down from his theater in Richmond for special engagements in the city, had been in the same cast a goodly number of times but never appeared in an important scene with her. At their infrequent meetings there were always jests about her introduction to Mr. Rich and his cats.

Other times Tom watched her from out front, never failing to delight in the radiance and freshness of this gem of femininity. She was intelligent, artistically superb and beautiful; lovely to see and hear, lovely in voice and gesture.

She had become the first lady of the London theater at a time when there were many giantesses of talent competing with her. Her characterization of Sir Harry Wildair in *The Constant Couple* was far beyond the expectations of old Rich. She performed the role twenty times the first season with such easy elegance and wit that it was said no male actor could ever equal her. So rapidly had her fame spread that members of royalty led the "repeaters" by coming to see the performance six times.

But, because of her success, her private affairs did not pass without censure. How much of the gossip was true and not merely sensationalism can not be judged, but we do know that once, when running off the stage in male costume to tumultuous applause, she said with a chuckle, "I do believe half the men out there are convinced I'm a man." To which crusty old Quin, standing in the wings, replied acidly, "And the other half know full well you're not." On one occasion the Duchess of Queensberry entered the Greenroom suddenly, and was petrified with horror at seeing Peg with a pot of porter held aloft, toasting *Confusion to All Order*.

She had been sought out by many men, talked about and scandalized in more ways than one; but still she remained London's favorite, and her later years, at least, were free from criticism. The tales told of her earlier years grew less and less adverse, until the *bad lady* became a legend. She had won and held the admiration and respect of all for twenty years.

During her last few performances Tom had thought he noticed a momentary clouding over of a facial expression which would have enlivened a point of speech, and a habit of grasping her side while on stage, without apparent motivation. Only a professional would notice such departures. So great was her art that the layman could not distinguish these things from a telling stage look or graceful gesture.

But now—Touchstone to her Rosalind!

Preparation for a big performance was always hard work, but so clearly and gently spoken were her instructions, and so keen was his own professional sense born of long training, that rehearsing with her was as soothing as the reading of a pleasant book. Like all good actors, he was intensely nervous before the first curtain, but once in front of the audience his lines and movements returned to him with the same smoothness and skill as in his rehearsals with her.

The play went on the boards before an enthusiastic audience. They were in no way disappointed. What a Rosalind she made! How attentive the crowd to every little point she put across to them! They loved her for this which she could do so well, and for two hours nothing else mattered.

Her spell carried behind the lights as well as beyond them and almost without the cast seeming to realize it, the play was drawing to its close. Tom had played his first scene with her, and now his second. He felt that he was topping any performance he had ever given as Touchstone, or as anything else for that matter. The charm of this woman would permit only a reading that was inspired.

Once during the performance he noticed a look of pain sweep across her face; several times he saw her clutch her side. But these alarming incidents momentarily forgotten, what joy he felt when *she* stood in the entrance and applauded as he came off from his "Seven Ages" speech!

And now it was all but over—all but the hand clapping and the curtain calls. The applause was deafening as the audience rose from their seats in unanimous acclaim.

Time after time the curtain rose for the company, time after time it rose for the individual artists. Tom's head swam with the knowledge that, next to her Rosalind, his Touchstone was most favored.

At last all was quiet for the epilogue.

Tom stood in the entrance on the opposite side. This was hers alone—a beautiful invention of the Elizabethan dramatists, and this by the master, an afterword in Shakespeare's own delicate hand.

The house was almost breathlessly still. Rosalind stood before the row of candles and looked the house over, the boxes, the rows of tiers, the pits. She was in complete command.

Then came the gracious smile. The beautiful voice had a clear, joyous quality flowing forth so effortlessly, so charmingly, so distinct.

It is not the fashion to see the lady the epilogue; but it is no more unhandsome than to see the lord the prologue. If it be true that good wine needs no bush, 'tis true that a good play needs no epilogue: yet to good wine they do use good bushes; and good plays prove the better by the help of good epilogues. What a case am I in then, that am neither a good epilogue, nor cannot insinuate with you in the behalf of a good play! I am not furnished like a beggar, therefore to beg will not become me: my way is to conjure you; and I'll begin with the women. I charge you, O women; for the love you bear to men, to like as much of this play as please you: and I charge you, O men, for the love you bear to women—as I perceive by your simpering, none of you hates them—that between you and the women the play may please. If I were a woman I would kiss as many of you as had beards that pleased me—

Suddenly—the clutch at her side; then not the words of *any* playwright but a strange guttural, "Oh, my God! Oh, my God!" She sank slowly to the stage.

Chapman rushed to the fallen actress, picked her up in his arms and carried her off stage.

He stopped for a moment there to look at her face. She seemed to try to smile and he thought he heard a whispered, "Exit, Elizabeth."

Tom moved quickly toward her dressing room, but before he reached the door he felt the body of Mistress Peg Woffington grow heavy and lifeless in his arms.

Plate 1

William Chapman Sr. in *Montrose*

Plate 2

William B. Chapman Jr. in *Cherry and Fair Star*

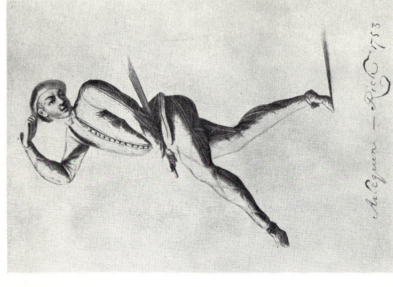

John Rich, originator of English pantomime

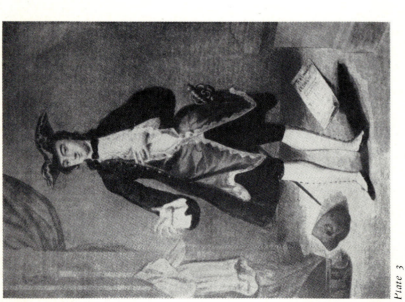

Peg Woffington in *Sir Harry Wildair*

*Thomas Chapman's Theatre, Richmond, England*

*Chapter 4*

# There's a Divinity

The well-filled years of a life were drawing to a close for Tom Chapman.

The theater in Richmond had seen its day. It was faded and barely serviceable but the massive oak in the garden was still strong and well. Beneath its boughs, in a padded chair, sat old Tom Chapman. A small boy rested at his feet, dozing against Tom's leg in the warm summer's sun.

Tom was not so old in years, and certainly not in appearance, but he knew that Time was beginning to make inroads. Many things warned him that he was going downhill fast.

It seemed but yesterday that he was striding through the juveniles at Covent Garden in London, reading his lines, taking his bows, hurrying home to Nora and the boys. But that only made the change more vivid. There were practical evidences, too. His two front teeth were loose; their loss would be irreparable to him as an actor. And though he disguised it from everyone, his hearing was failing as well. He was missing cues every night now. He picked up most of the lost ones by watching the positions, gestures and facial expressions of his fellow actors. He had memorized the roles, having rotated his stock of plays so many times.

From his earliest days on the stage his sturdy legs had been a source of pride to him, but they seemed unsteady now, and his ankles were swollen after long performances. His days of wearing tights were over.

Although it was warm, he was trembling. The most frightening thing was that he could never again study a part, because his eyes were failing him. He would awake to find them bloodshot and only constant hot bathing relieved the stinging that was always there. Blindness ran in the family and, in his case, the optic injury he had suffered in the war had helped to hasten it.

Moreover, he had lost his ability to retain lines. About forty of his parts, particularly the ones he had learned in the early years of his professional life, were clearly written in the tablets of his memory; but, in addition to the trouble with his eyes, he had not been able to memorize a single side of twenty lines for more than a year. Sadly he realized he would never create another role.

What, then, was there to live for? The past? It had

been glorious and pleasurable to look back upon. It canceled out those hard years of war. And, the great women of the theater: Woffington, Bracegirdle, Sentos, Clive. Never again would they be equaled. The new actresses, interesting as they were, could not grasp the great sweep and dignity of the old parts. And what men came from the old school! Spranger Barry, whose voice was like music; and that energetic little fellow, Garrick—bustle, bustle, bustle, it's true, but his tragedy had them sitting on the edge of their chairs and his comedy made the whole house rock. Quin, Delaine, Ryan—great men and great actors. It was singular that so much of this talent came from Ireland.

The world of the theater as he had known it was gone. What then remained?

His family? Nora had died long ago. What a companion she had been; the memory of her was with him every hour still, but it did not provide the solace of human warmth which his old age required.

His two sons then? One, a handsome blond lad, had died fighting with Braddock in far-off America. A life, thought Tom, wasted on a wilderness. His other son, at an early age, had married the daughter of a rich man of trade. The father-in-law had opposed the union from the start, and the boy had been lost at sea, the ship never heard from. Although they had had a child, his capricious wife had almost immediately involved herself in an elopement to the Continent. A fine sense of respect to the recent dead! A fine sense of duty to the living! She had not wanted to have the child in tow to interfere with her new love life.

So all that was left of Tom's direct line was the son of

this misguided marriage. The lad was now five years old and treasured by the old man. He boarded the boy with actor friends at Covent Garden. One day each week was all he could have of him now; each moment was precious. The boy who dozed at Tom's feet was his last link with the world, and a new life for *the profession*.

There was something to live for. Reveries were over; to work then.

" 'Arouse ye, arouse ye, my merry Swiss boy,' " sang Tom.

Little Will Chapman stirred. He rubbed his eyes and shook his curls.

"Come, grandson," said the old gentleman. "Time to show me what you've learned. 'The Douglas Speech,' they tell me. Let's have it."

The boy stood up quickly and took an heroic stance.

" 'My name is Norval; On the Campanian hills my father feeds his flocks; A frugal swain, Whose constant cares were to increase his store, And keep his only son, myself, at home. . . .' "

"Not so fast, not so fast!" broke in the elder. "More light and shade, my boy. More light and—"

A shadow appeared on the ground before them. They looked up.

A portly looking man finely accoutered in a severe, somewhat clerical garb stood by.

"Still at it, Tom, I see," he said.

Chapman nodded, and spoke to the boy. "Run to Mrs. Sanky's and bring back Blanche. I'll be busy for a while."

"Don't you want to hear the rest of the speech?" said the lad. "I've taken great pains with it." Tom shook his head.

The boy ran off around the side of the theater.

"I've come again, Tom," said the gentleman, "and for the last time in kindness. He's my grandson, too, you know."

"You've had my answer before," replied Tom. "I don't have to repeat my reasons, but I will. You were against my son's marriage from the very first. You did everything you could to bring it to disaster. You ridiculed the profession he could have followed and drove him instead to seek a life on the sea. We know what happened. And you! You married off your daughter again as quickly after his disappearance as you could, even before it was sure his ship was lost. An elopement they called it!"

"This is not a discussion of my character," said the other man. "We're talking about what is best for the boy, and surely this is not...."

Tom broke in again. "You took no notice of him for three years, not a thought did you give him until, just by chance, you happened to see what a beauty he is. You wanted him then. You even tried to buy him. But I have him now and I'll keep him. He's *all* I have, Mr. Alsop Archdeacon."

"Yes, I want him and I'll get him," retorted the merchant. "And no slurs on religion, if you please. The fact that I support the church is just another reason why I should have the boy. You haven't been to meeting for four months. You'll regret it some December morning when we bury you in the cold ground of yonder churchyard. It won't be long either. You're getting on. You don't look it, but you're at least ten years older than I. God knows how you manage to conceal your age!"

"I'll tell you the secret," said the actor. "I change my wine and women often."

"Fool!" sputtered the pompous churchman. "What

has that to do with it? But to get back to the boy. Can
you have him educated? How will you pay for it? I
know your financial condition. This shack of a theater
isn't making a penny. Not that it ever made anything but
a lot of noise. You haven't had as much as half a house
for the past six months. I saw three principals of your
company leave for London this morning, baggage and
all. You owe money to everyone in town. Covent Garden
sends for you no longer. You won't last another month."

"I've always paid my bills," said Tom, "and my theater will be a theater if I have to play here alone. The
people who left this morning went as my friends. They'll
be standing at the churchyard when I'm put away, and
many more. The theater of London won't forget Thomas
Chapman, comedian, nor will the *Gazette* let that happen.
And if it comes to finding new actors, I'll find them. I'll
make actors. There are very few people whom I can't
teach how to act."

"So you're starting in on the boy?" said the gentleman. "You'd have him live a life like yours and come
to an end like this. You close your mind to what I can
give him, and think it's enough to teach him to perform
like a trained dog. Very well, I'll see that you are ruined.
You shall not have a single nut to crack. I'll have the law
on you, man!"

Tom nodded, unperturbed. "We've gone over all that,
too. I know all about your wealth and high moral position; but what about your daughter's behavior while
married to my son? And you! Do you think, with that
fine North Country tongue, that you're as educated as
I? Ask anyone in town." Tom shook his head. "No. The
boy has my name and he'll keep it. He'll choose his own

way of life, and I think I know what that will be. You hated my son, but you want his boy. Oh, no, Mr. Moneybags! Once a Chapman always a Chapman, and that's his name."

"He may have your name," replied the other, indignation searing his words, "but he's also flesh of my flesh and bone of my bone, and I'll take him away from you. You and your cardboard people worked on wires, saying whatever is put into your mouths. God, what a life for a grandson of mine!"

"Here comes the boy again," said the actor gently. "Kindly leave."

Alsop reddened with frustration, turned and moved forward to plant himself in the boy's way.

"Here, my lad," he said, "is a half crown. See what you can do with it. And remember, there's much more for you in good time."

With that, he strutted off.

"Bring the coin here, grandson," said Tom. "Give it to me."

Will did so.

"You know what this is, don't you?" asked Tom.

Will nodded.

"It's money. A half crown," said Tom. "It's probably honest money, honestly earned; but it's not honest for you to take it or spend it."

"I did not take it, grandfather," said William with some bewilderment. "Is it not a gift to me?"

"It was the giving of it that was not honest," replied Tom. "You must always beware of such unexpected kindnesses. Something for nothing is seldom altogether honest."

"Then," said Will, "what am I to do with it?"

"I'll tell you. You know the old beggar woman who sits by the pillar at Covent Garden?" The boy nodded. "Well, when you come next week I want you to tell me that you have given this half crown to the old lady— all as a secret between you and me."

"I will do just as you say," said William as he pocketed the money and then stood looking at Tom, a warm sun in the dusk of the old man's life. "Blanche said I was to meet her at the stage coach as soon as I had said farewell to you."

Tom embraced him, the boy kissed his cheek and ran off waving good-bye.

Alone, Tom threw back his head and gazed into the blue sky, his arms outstretched before him with palms upturned. It was one of his most effective stage gestures. I mustn't do this, he thought. More and more often of late he caught himself striking these positions off stage. All actors of advanced years did that.

He arose from his chair and picked up his hat from the ground, grunting audibly as he did so. He did not like that either. He had used such a trick often in playing feeble old men on the stage, but now it was real.

Slowly he made his way through the theater to his dressing room and lit the candle. Two hours before playing time—another shock! It was an axiom that the older the actor the earlier he came to the theater.

From the pegs about his cracked mirror he took several wigs, looked them over and gave each a dressing. When he had replaced them he removed the one he was wearing and began to comb it. It was truly blond, the same bright color and glitter as his own hair had been the day, years ago, he had offered it for sale to Mr. Rich's wigmaker. Then he looked into the mirror and sighed deeply at the sight of his shining bald pate.

He made up and dressed in his costume for the evening performance. He looked into the mirror again, straightened his shoulders, and with something of his old military carriage, climbed the creaking stairs to the stage.

A single candle burned on the edge of the stage. Its feeble but beautiful glow softened everything it touched. That was well, for this *was* a tawdry looking place, and Tom knew it. Still, it was a theater and his own. Fine word, "his": his place, his watch, his ring and his knee buckle, the last a present from Nora.

The stage and the dressing room housed the tools of his trade. On that rack over there were *his* towers; their splendor had long since peeled off with the paint, but still they were his own . . . he had used those pieces for his temple scenes, too. On the opposite stack was his palace scene; ah, his gorgeous palace! All his, every bit of it. This was his world, his great globe.

But nevertheless, it was disheartening. This was all he had to leave the boy. All, and yet it was nothing. He would die and William would be too young to make use of the little he would leave.

He moved slowly, unself-consciously to where the candle threw its brightest light. He began to speak. The voice was still there! It had been there in barns, at the fairs, and at the great theater in London. It would always be there, for any role from sixteen to sixty! It would be there as long as he had being.

So thus buoyed and inspired, he began:

71

Our revels now are ended. These our actors,
As I foretold you, were all spirits, and
Are melted into air, into thin air:
And, like the baseless fabric of this vision,
The cloud-capp'd towers, the gorgeous palaces,
The solemn temples, the great globe itself,
Yea, all which it inherit, shall dissolve,
And, like this insubstantial pageant faded,
Leave not a rack behind. We are such stuff
As dreams are made of; and our little life
Is rounded with sleep. . . .

There was the sound of clapping from a corner somewhere in the darkness. It was Alec, the man who cleaned
the theater.

"Afore God, Governor," he said, "that was beautiful,
just beautiful! There's no reader in the country can hold
a candle to you. But why now? You're up in it and it's
long before curtain time."

"Practice, Alec, just practice," said Prospero. "We
actors must never let down, you know. We must make
constant use of our gifts. After all, as Sweet William
says, it's 'a little life.' "

*Exterior, Covent Garden Theatre*

## Chapter 5

# Fine Word, Legitimate

Will Chapman continued to board with Tom's friends at Covent Garden for another year, until his grandfather died. Will was six then and his maternal grandfather, Alsop, the rich merchant, took possession of him and sent him to school. During vacations he was privately tutored and instructed in the ways of the rich and well-born.

But the promise of wealth and position faded when this grandsire passed on, for the family, not wishing to share their inheritance, now let the world kidnap the boy sixteen years old. He and his belongings were set out upon the sidewalk, and, like Will Shakespeare of old, he made his way to his friends in the theater.

Tom Chapman's few remaining old cronies, most especially the stage manager, Mr. Harris, bade Will an actor's welcome and he was put to work. He was a slim blond youth and the first part that fell to his lot was Slender, in Shakespeare's *Merry Wives of Windsor*.

A character actor does not thrive on top billing, but on lending the best and most rounded support to any lead to which he is assigned. And a good actor of this type can, without ostentation, outshine the stars. As a character actor Will Chapman began, and a character actor he remained throughout his long career.

His theatrical path crossed those of the great and near-great in the theater of his time. One such near-great was Master William Henry West Betty.

The parents of this boy took him, when he was eleven years of age, to the theater in Belfast to see Mrs. Siddons as Evadne in the play of the same name. Master Betty bought himself a copy of the play the next day; two days after that he had memorized the part. From then on he out-Siddoned Mrs. Siddons in the declamatory fireworks of that loud and ponderous role. He set the entire household on edge with it morning, noon and night. In later days he would have been taken to a doctor or a psychiatrist; but his parents took him to the stage door instead.

There they met a Mr. Haugh, the prompter of the company. A prompter in those days was a man who "knew the book." That is, he was supposed to know the lines of all the standard classic dramatic plays of the time and be able to teach quickly the comedies and afterpieces, songs included. Mr. Haugh heard the boy read

Evadne and found him a phenomenon. With this boy, the prompter saw an opportunity of getting into London, as much the goal of all thespians then as it is now.

Young Betty had a mind like a sponge and a prodigious memory. He could read a page and repeat it with closed eyes, and no piece of stage business had to be shown him more than once. That first season Haugh taught the lad six leading parts and he played them with such success that reports of it reached the metropolis. From Belfast he was engaged by the shrewd Macready for Manchester. Two weeks before the opening Macready's feet began to cool and he asked for an adjustment of the terms, which called for Betty to receive ten pounds a performance. Macready's suggestion was that the first sixty pounds go for the overhead, the straight regular expense of the theater; anything over that the manager and the star were to share equally. The new terms resulted in Master Betty getting fifty instead of ten pounds each night and the report of this also reached London in a day or two.

The next engagement was at Edinburgh. The opening bill was *Douglas* with Betty playing the part of Norval. The author, seventy-year-old John Home, had heard the most distinguished actors of the age speak his lines. He sat in the wings throughout the play and at the fall of the last curtain he rushed on stage to take the bows with the star. More than that, he made a speech affirming that the part had never been better played. And, naturally, what he did and said was heard in London in no time at all.

John Philip Kemble was compelled to book the boy into the leading London theater, Covent Garden. William Chapman's name can be found on several bills with that of *Young Roscius*. For Betty's opening program at Covent Garden, the entrances to the theater were besieged before noon by people clamoring for admission. By the time the doors were opened, people were fighting, fainting, screeching; many were severely injured. After every performance, dozens of carriages were waiting, hoping to carry him off to various engagements.

The receipts are on record and it is hard to believe them. The boy received fifty guineas a performance and the take averaged the unprecedented sum of six hundred pounds a night. When the engagement started the theater was a half-year behind in rent; when it ended, the theater was a half-year ahead. In addition to the Shakespearean roles of Romeo and Hamlet, Master Betty appeared in seven other leading classic parts.

Betty's engagement for the second season was something else. The receipts were cut in half and the actors began to revolt. During the first engagement Kemble had surrounded the boy with all the actors of small stature he could find, but for the second season the male members of the company were all well over six feet. So humiliated were the actors over appearing with this child of limited acting ability that time and again they pleaded illness rather than appear.

One of the most talented men of the company, a Mr. Hargrave, was cast one night as second lead to Master Betty. Shortly before the opening curtain the prompter announced that Mr. Hargrave had suddenly withdrawn himself from the company and could not be found. It was afterward learned that he had gone back into the army from which he had come. He declared later that he had loved his profession, until the idiocy of the Betty vogue.

After a few seasons in the provinces, Master Betty grew up and went through the University with honor. But when, as a full-grown man, he returned to the London stage, it was found that although he had matured physically, his talent had diminished. He retired and lived comfortably for the rest of his life on his earnings as a child.

But there were, indeed, far more substantial showmen in the theater of William Chapman's day. There have been several claimants to divine right of dynasty in the history of the theater, but no family ever acted the part as did the Kembles.

The descendants of this family who have been in the theater extend down to the present time, but only two members, John Philip Kemble and Sarah Siddons, had any influence on the fortunes of the Chapmans.

The Kembles' theatrical history began with a provincial manager, Roger Kemble, whose stubborn stand was that none of his children should tread the boards. With this edict in view, Roger's offspring were most carefully educated; the males sent to the college at Douay with the avowed intent of becoming Catholic priests. However, none of them ever wore the cloth except on the stage.

At first the Kemble clan had a struggle to get established in the metropolis, but once they were in the limelight they took good care to stay in the center of the glare. They adopted the mannerisms of the aristocrats, and these roles they played on the stage and off. John Philip's favorite character was that of Coriolanus, throughout which he could view the plebeians with condescension. Sarah was in her glory when she donned her most queenly robe to be painted by Sir Joshua Reynolds as the Tragic Muse. The most devoted admirers of Mrs. Siddons had to admit that even in the privacy of her home she lacked refined manners. She made a studied effort to insure that her bearing at all times was as queenly and dramatic as the appearance she made on the stage. She could not tolerate physical imperfections. When Sarah played Rosalind she wore a jacket long enough to cover her knees. It was rumored that she was against revealing the female form. As a matter of fact, she was tragically bowlegged. Great care had to be taken with the furniture of the sets which she used. On one important occasion in London, the set had been built so close to specifications that one of the critics noted "when she rose the chair rose with her."

John Kemble, clad in white stockings and thin pumps, strutted through the drawing rooms of the elite and the rehearsals at the theater as though he were the guiding spirit of both domains. He wore "fats" on his long, thin shanks and even his Roman togas had to be made to hide as much of him as possible. In Sir Thomas Lawrence's painting of him as Rolla there is scarcely a toga or any other article of clothing to be seen; but only the head of this famous painting is of Kemble. The muscular physique is that of the champion heavyweight prizefighter of the day, Tom Sayers.

The Kembles were great artists in the eyes of the fashionable audiences of their time and ruled supreme for many years, but even so, John's first triumphs were at Drury Lane. After years of success there he bought a one-sixth interest in Covent Garden and moved over to assume complete charge. Never was an age or a city

more fitted for what the Kembles had to sell. The aristocracy purchased box seats for the season long before the
doors were open. Triumph followed triumph until, at
four o'clock the morning of September 18, 1808, the
house caught fire and burned to the ground within ten
hours. The loss to the family was staggering. All of their
theatrical equipment and much of their personal property
went up in flames. The accumulation of many years of
hard work—costumes, jewelry, scenery, music and scripts
—were lost forever. The city itself was in profound
mourning, for fifteen firemen were lost and many others
injured in the futile attempt to save the burning structure.

The Kembles were in deep despair; all except John
who lost no time in showing his ingenuity. Within a
fortnight he was at work raising funds for a new and
greater theater. The response from the aristocracy was
magnificent. The Duke of Northumberland came forward with a loan of ten thousand pounds and canceled
the debt the day the cornerstone was laid. Money poured
in from every source and within a year the greatest London theater ever built, Covent Garden, was ready to
open.

The tragedy of *Macbeth* was announced with John
and Sarah in the leading roles. Beneath the cast announcement on the program was a statement to the effect that
the building costs of this new civic treasure had been extremely high and that it would be some time before
the theater could pay for itself. Beneath this was a list
of the prices. The pit and the box seats were to be raised
a shilling. Surely there was every justice in that; but it
also appeared that there was a distinct change in the

architecture of the second-tier seats: twenty-four boxes had been built, equipped with anterooms where refreshments could be served. The boxes had already been sold for the season at the exceedingly high price of 400 pounds. The upper galleries, which traditionally were occupied by citizens of small means and drama-loving apprentices of the city, were now so steeply pitched that only half the stage could be seen. Over the places where the lavish private boxes had been built, the galleries had been cut up into small cubbyholes. Five patrons had to strain to peer through this "window" as it was derisively called.

Before the building was completed the huge advance sale of the private boxes, the unprecedented rise in the prices and the faulty construction of the top galleries had become the talk of the town. A nerve in the pocketbook of the general public had been touched to the quick. There was an audible murmur of protest throughout the city, but the Kembles did not trouble themselves about it. Indeed, so great was the excitement for the opening that those connected with it were totally deaf to the threat: "Britons never shall be slaves."

After the great green curtain had been drawn everyone rose and sang the national anthem in his best voice, but no sooner had Mr. Kemble appeared to deliver the dedication than, along with the waves of applause, there began a steady undertone of hisses. This shocking thing might have been personal venom of the apprentices against the aristocratic John; but when the curtain rose on Macbeth and Duncan many of the patrons climbed onto their seats, turned their backs to the curtain and began to shout, "Off! Off! No new prices. No new

prices!" The shouts and the applause continued throughout the play. Scarcely a word from the actors could be
heard. . . . The "O.P. Riots" had begun. In the present
jargon of the theater, the gala opening had "laid an egg"
and King John had "got the bird."

The next day London buzzed with the disgraceful
affair. Nothing was said in defense of the belligerents
even though they greatly outnumbered the ones who
had paid high prices for their box seats. As the nights
went on the tumult increased.

John Philip Kemble became a fair target for the
crowd's scorn. In his speeches to the noisy audience his
tone was far from conciliatory and only incensed them
further. Ignoring the polite phrase, "What might be
your pleasure," he bluntly demanded to know "what
they wanted." Answering yells came back in language
too vulgar to print here, and banners bearing a similar
text were stretched across the house on lines let down
from the balconies. The crowd's hostility was not confined within the walls of the theater; in the privacy of
their pubs they bitterly continued to castigate the great
man's acting and even his pronunciation, and to loudly
bawl that the anterooms of the second balcony boxes
were used for purposes other than that of serving refreshments.

On Kemble's suggestion, the theater was closed for a
few nights while a committee of prominent men went
over the books to show that the backers of the new house
were receiving but a poor rate of interest on their invest-
ment. This made no difference to the rowdy opposition
so long as they could point to the fact that Mrs. Siddons
was receiving fifty guineas a night.

The theater was reopened, but the pandemonium was all the greater. The "Old Prices Dance" began: singing and wild dancing went on up and down the aisles while the actors, lined up in desperation behind the footlights, tried to shout their lines above the tumult. Many of the rioters were seized by the constabulary and thrown into jail until the following day. But the released rioters returned the next evening or were quickly replaced by others.

Acting with John Philip at this time was George Frederick Cooke, whom many considered to be Kemble's equal. He had a strong, well-shaped body, a classic face, blazing eyes and a beautiful, resonant voice. This last gift was something that Mr. Kemble sadly lacked. But Cooke also had another attribute—a great thirst. During his many years in the theater he hardly ever drew a sober breath for more than two consecutive days. Often he came on the stage scarcely able to walk or talk and as often, he was hissed off. The evening after the humiliations he would give such a magnificent performance that the hisses were turned into cheers. Doubtless he was one of the greatest actors on the English stage. John Philip Kemble was the pet of the aristocracy and the intellectuals, but George Frederick Cooke was the darling of the workers and the crowd. He would sit in the taverns far into the night and say that, given a scene with Kemble where the parts were of equal importance, he could make "Black Jack tremble in his pumps."

Since most of the venom seemed to be directed to Kemble, it was thought by the investors that the revolt would be broken if "The King" absented himself and allowed the pride of the gallery, Mr. Cooke, to take over as star of the performance. The role selected for Cooke was that of Sir Pertinax MacSycophant in *The Man of the World*, a part which Kemble himself said George could not be equaled in by any actor past or present.

When Cooke made his entrance, cold sober this time, there was round after round of hearty applause, but when he started his first speech the roars broke out and his performance was reduced to a series of graceful gestures. The banners were brought forth as usual and now they read:

> Cooke we pity;
> Kemble we despise.

Then the proprietors of the house made their last, fatal mistake. They created a police force of their own by hiring a noted heavyweight bruiser and his stable of pugilists to spread themselves among the crowd and silence every disturber they could find. The fights created more noise and drew more attention from the stage than had the "O.P. Dance."

Finally, after nearly three months, King John had to climb down from his high horse, put the prices back to the O.P. scale, take down the private boxes and their anterooms, and remodel the upper galleries. By that time the boxes had been empty for many nights. Most of the actors in the original cast had drifted away; Cooke had used some of them on a tour of the provinces, others had gone to smaller London theaters or jobs in nontheatrical fields. Their places were filled as best as possible. It mattered very little. No proper performance had been given for ten weeks.

But there was one Kemble man on the program who was loyal to King John from first to last. He played Duncan at the opening of the theater, his name was on the program for the final performance of the "O.P. Riots," and it was listed again when the theater re-opened at the old prices. That man was William Chapman.

Like his grandfather, the theater had not only given William his career, but a wife as well. In 1805 a celebrated Irish actress, Penelope Britt, joined the Co-vent Garden Theatre. Her career started brilliantly in Edinburgh as Nora in *A Maid of all Work*, but she gave it all up to marry William who was then a member of the company. They had four sons, William, Samuel, Bernard and George, and two daughters, Sarah and Terese.

Will, the eldest, was the old man's favorite and the first of the clan to cross the ocean for the New World. By the time he was sixteen, William's namesake had played *the boy* to Sarah Siddons and other leading theater artists of the day. When he was eighteen he left the family to be on his own and quickly became a leading actor of robust male roles in the principal cities of England. Success had come easily to him and with that a taste for the rakish, a trait which was a source of grievance to his parents.

Young Will's wardrobe and wig collection were the envy of all actors. One Turkish costume was a mass of paste diamonds, emeralds, rubies and pearls and he wore it as though he were a born potentate of the East. From top to toe he sparkled and this, coupled with his mother's wit, made him a redoubtable fellow with the girls. At the age of twenty, it was certain he would become one of London's favorite actors.

One night he entered the famous house in Bow Street as the curtain was about to rise, went to the dressing room of his father and burst in with his usual show of exuberance.

"Greetings, sire," he said, holding out a silk purse.

His father was seated at his make-up table. He glanced at his son, then went on with his preparations.

Young Will dangled the silk purse for his father's attention. "Here's help with the rent and victuals," he said.

"You've been successful, I see," said the senior, "but you'd best hold that until you hear what I have to say."

"Oh, I'm doing all right," Will replied. "I've played every county in England and created a sensation in every town. I have several engagements lined up and won't need this."

"You'll need it," said his father, with emphasis. "I'll tell you why."

"But the performance. . . ?"

"I'm not in this act until later. There's time for what I have to say."

"If you're thinking I should stay closer to home," said Will, "I can have London, but I don't need it. Read these." He handed his father a batch of newspaper clippings. "I've made enough for an entire new set of costumes and wigs. Everything new, on stage and off."

"I take your boasting to mean that you think you're quite a success?"

"Well—yes," said Will, a bit uncomfortable.

"And the ladies?" said his father. "You're a success with them too?"

"A man doesn't talk about that," said the young spark. "I have a way, I admit. But why a note like this?" He took a small piece of paper from his sleeve cuff and read, " 'Come in the front way with the audience. Do not speak to anyone and move quickly.' What's the mystery?"

"It's here," said his father. From under his make-up table he drew out a small basket and removed a woolen covering.

There, lying peacefully asleep, was a tiny baby.

"I've warned you again and again," the elder man intoned. "I've asked you to respect your family, if not yourself, and this is your answer! The child was left in this dressing room tonight. I came in first, luckily. No one here knows."

"It's a fair babe," said his son, peering at it with his head cocked to one side. "A beautiful child, in fact."

"And its mother?"

"I never take down a lady's history," said gentleman Will. "All they need tell me is that they love me. I look upon these things as an adventure. And truly," he bragged, "it's hard indeed for a man to feel ashamed of a product such as this!"

"You'll be more frightened than proud when you read the note that came with it. Here," his father handed him a small sheet of paper that had been lying on the table.

"This seems to be the night for notes," said Will and read, " 'For this birth there shall now be a death.' " The bravado faded. His face turned white.

"Note the word *now*," said his father. "I see that you recognize the signature. The most dangerous man in England today. He and his ruffians have murdered for ten years without spending one day in jail. And as for his daughter, well . . . 'Hell hath no fury like a woman scorned.' An adventure!" he mocked. "Indeed, the most exciting scene is yet to be played. Now listen. There were men waiting for you at the stage door, there are men at the front of the house, and there's a spy in the company here. As soon as the final curtain falls they will go to work."

Though his coloring was returning, it was evident that Will realized the seriousness of his position. He wet his lips but could not speak.

"The last scene of this play is dark," his father went on, "and as the curtain falls you are to stand on the trap behind the backdrop upstage right. Prentice will let you down and close the trap again. Find your way in the dark to the orchestra pit and pass into the audience. Go toward the Weymouth docks, mixing with the crowd as long as you can. You'll be safe until you reach Mile End Road. From there to the docks is the danger stretch. Keep your hand on your sword. You know how to use it."

"But at Weymouth dock, what?"

"There you will find the *Charming Sally*, bound for America."

"America?" Will repeated.

"America. I have sent a messenger to arrange your passage. When you reach the other side, let us hear. Remember now all I have told you. Be ready to 'act' at the end of the play. In the meantime, do not leave this room."

"I understand," said Will. "I . . . good-bye." He put out his hand.

"Well, good luck, my boy," Will Sr. pressed his hand. "There's my cue," he said abruptly and left the dressing room without another word.

Will now had two hours in which to look at his daughter and resolve to mend his ways. He was not valiant except upon the stage. There he could play the brave and noble hero to perfection, but he had small stomach for this sort of arrangement in real life. He thought he had side-stepped the issue very neatly, but the issue was very much alive. Furthermore, he had had the fun, but it was his father who had to bear the responsibility.

When the final curtain fell, Will took his place by the trap and was lowered into the pit. This was well indeed, for within a minute two rough-looking fellows made their way through the stage door and were slyly searching for something in every corner.

Guided by sound, he felt his way out of the pit and into the audience. As his father had predicted, the crush was so great that no one with hostile intentions could possibly spot him.

The crowd gradually thinned out and soon he was hurrying along the darkness, alone. When he reached the Mile End Road and looked down the long dark stretch ahead his nerve almost failed him, but there was no turning back now. He used his *entrance* walk to plunge ahead.

About halfway to the docks his ear told him he was being followed. Looking back, he could discern two hulking figures on either side of the street. Obviously, they were stalking him. And he still had half a mile to go!

He walked faster. On both sides of the street before him he thought he could see two other figures closing in on him stealthily. Hemmed in—surrounded, by thunder!

There were no side alleys here, no doors he might break in, if there were, he couldn't see them. He was trapped for sure. Four to one! If he should cry out no one would hear him and they would close in all the more quickly.

The pair who followed him were close now and the voice of one rang out, "Stand!"

Will drew his sword and turned to face them. Although outnumbered, he would fight; if he could get to the other side of them he could take to his heels and make his way back from where he had come. But the men who had led the way suddenly materialized on either side of him with faces masked and swords drawn. They confronted the villains who had been trailing him. He realized it was now three to two with the odds in his favor!

One of the ruffians at his side was the first to speak. It was a seaman's voice, such as mates use when bellowing to men up on the yards.

"Hold there!" it ordered. "We'll take this prize!"

The weapon in the hand of each crossed the swords of the highwaymen opposite them. Now Will joined the fray. From behind he gave one of his opponents such a stab in the buttocks that he jumped a good half foot into the air and turned to run howling back into town. When the sword of his other foe was sent ringing to the street, Will picked it up and hurled it to the roof of the nearby warehouse. This rogue also raced off in the same direction. What they told the "most dangerous man in England" with the wronged daughter is not recorded.

With his most effectively theatrical "Ha! Ha!" Will turned to thank his new-found friends. But as he started to speak they began to beat him with the flat of their swords and drive him toward the docks.

"Shanghaied, by God!" Will muttered as his mind flashed back to his comfortable past and his gorgeous Turkish costume.

Scuffling, panting, swearing, they arrived at the gangplank to a small ship. There the two men removed their masks and the surprised boy looked into the faces of his two younger brothers, Sam and George. Their laughter was loud as they cried out each other's name and embraced.

Then a rough voice boomed out from the ship, "Aboard there! We've been waiting for you and must cast off!"

For a moment there was silence. The two brothers could see that Will was crying like a child. This was a moment for comedy relief before the exit.

George took one of the hands of his brother Will, Sam took the other. Together they spoke their farewell.

> Forever and forever, farewell, William!
> If we do meet again, why, we shall smile;
> If not, why then, this parting was well made.

And right on cue Will replied:

> Forever and forever, farewell, Samuel.
> If we do meet again, we'll smile indeed;
> If not, 'tis true this parting was well made.

And still on cue, a voice from shipboard rang out, "Come ho, away there!" and Will Chapman walked up the plank, later to appear as a leading actor in the rising cities of America—Philadelphia, New York, Albany—in the camps of the gold-rush hordes and in the great palmy days of the theater in San Francisco.

*Interior, Theatre Royal, Bath, England*

*Chapter 6*

# What's in a Name?

By 1810, London had become a flourishing theatrical
town. Seven theaters were competing for the floating
shillings, and acting had become a respectable profession. There were more good actors than ever before.
Four months of the year they toured the towns which
surrounded London—new theaters were rising in all
thriving cities of England—or played the fairs, where the
theater had become the most important attraction. The
young, ambitious actors in the provinces were able to
see well-known performers in all their important roles.

The plays of Shakespeare were still the measure of their talents.

But the age was not without trouble and discomforts. Prices were high. Actors complained of the cost of living; proprietors of theaters complained of costs. Thespians insisted that they needed a pound four shillings to live through the week, and managers swore they would have to close if the individual salaries went a penny over a pound. Admission fees had inched up and the public had been in a general state of rebellion over the rising prices for three full years.

All this made but small impression on young Sam Bryant. His training as a churchman at Oxford had made him mistrust the theater. He had never seen a play; he had been to London only a few times. Once, at a small inn there, he had met a likeable young fellow, George Colman, who talked much of actors and plays and who was the author of several minor comedies.

One night Colman had an order on Covent Garden. Would Sam go along? Bryant hesitated but he was lonely and after the necessary amount of persuasion from George, he decided to go.

He witnessed a revelation. He sat through the play in a strange rapture and when flights of angels sang Hamlet to his rest, Sam made a silent vow that one day he would have a strong hand in this agreeable work. Colman took him behind the scenes and introduced him to Ophelia, a Miss Fisher, and Sam took another silent oath that he would win her even if he had to become an actor to do it. He realized that in one brief evening the Devil had taken possession of the Man of God. And it was, in many respects, a wonderful feeling.

New Theatre Royal, Beaufort Square, Bath.

WILL OPEN this present SATURDAY, OCTOBER 12, 1805;

# KING RICHARD III,

With entire new Scenery, Dresses, Machinery and other Decorations.

RICHARD, DUKE OF GLOSTER - - - - BY A GENTLEMAN
(His First Appearance on the Stage)
KING HENRY THE SIXTH - - - - MR. CHARLTON
PRINCE OF WALES - - - - MISS MARTIN
DUKE OF YORK - - - - - MISS L. QUICK
DUKE OF BUCKINGHAM - - - - MR. CAULFIELD
(From the Theatre Royal, Drury Lane, His First Appearance on the Bath Stage)
DUKE OF NORFOLK - - - - - MR. EGAN
EARL OF OXFORD - - - - - - MR. ABBOTT
HENRY EARL OF RICHMOND - - - - MR. EGERTON
LORD STANLEY - - - - - MR. RICHARDSON
(His First appearance here these three years)
LORD MAYOR OF LONDON - - - - MR. EVANS
SIR W. BRANDON - - - - MR. CUNNINGHAM
SIR RICHARD RATCLIFFE - - - - MR. CUSHING
(His first appearance here)
SIR WILLIAM CATESBY     | SIR JAMES BLUNT
     MR. GOMERY |     MR. EDWARD
SIR R. BRACKENBURY | DIGHTON    MR. LODGE
     MR. GATTIE | FOREST     MR. SIMS
SIR JAMES TYRELL   MR. KELLY |
QUEEN ELIZABETH - - - - - MISS FISHER
DUCHESS OF YORK - - - - MRS. CHARLTON
LADY ANNE - - - - - MISS JAMESON
The Scenes by Messrs. Greaves, Marchbank, French and Capon,
The Dresses by Mr. Chuck and assistants—The female Dresses by Mrs. Jefferies.

*Plate 5*

Program with Miss Fisher (Mrs. Wm. Chapman Sr.)

NEW THEATRE ROYAL, COVENT-GARDEN,
This present THURSDAY, Nov. 15, 1810, will be acted Shakspeare's Tragedy of

# M A C B E T H.

The Overtures and Symphonies between the Acts by Mr WARE—The Vocal Musick by Matthew Lock
Duncan, King of Scotland, by Mr. CHAPMAN,
Malcolm by Mr. CLAREMONT, Donalbain by Mr. MENAGE,
Macbeth by Mr. KEMBLE, Macduff by Mr. C. KEMBLE,
Banquo by Mr. MURRAY, Fleance by Master CHAPMAN,
Lenox by Mr. CRESWELL, Rosse by Mr. EGERTON,
Siward Mr ATKINS, Seyton Mr JEFFERIES, Physician Mr DAVENPORT
Officers, Mess. King & Lambert, Chamberlains, Mess. Heath & Truman
Gentlemen, Mess. Brown, Gaywood, Grant, Louis, Powers, Sarjant,
Lady Macbeth by Mrs. SIDDONS,
Gentlewoman by Mrs HUMPHRIES,
Hecat' by Mr BELLAMY, Witches, Mess. BLANCHARD, FARLEY, SIMMONS
Apparitions, Mr. Field, Miss S. Goodwin, Miss C. Goodwin.
*The Choral Witches by*
Mess. I. Bellamy, Bishop, Bond, Burden, Dixon, Drofet, Everard, Fairclough, Hickman, Lee, Linton, Norris
Odwell, Sawyer, Street, Taylor, Terry, Tett, Tinney, Treby, Williams—Mesdames Bolton, Coates, Emery
Fawcett, Fenwick. Findlay, Grimaldi, Hardy, Iliff, Leferve, Lifton, Logan, Price, Watts, Whitmore.
To which will be added (by permission of the Proprietors of the Theatre Royal, Haymarket) the Farce of

# The VILLAGE LAWYER.

Justice Mittimus by Mr. DAVENPORT, Scout by Mr. FAWCETT,
Snarl, Mr. BLANCHARD, Charles, Mr. MENAGE,
Sheepface by Mr. EMERY, Clerk by Mr. SARJANT,
Constables, Mess. Louis & Powers,
Mrs. Scout, Mrs. DAVENPORT, Kate, Miss FENWICK.
Boxes 7s. Second Price 3s 6d.—Pit 3s 6d. Second Price 2s.
Lower Gallery 2s. Second Price 1s—Upper Gallery 1s. Second Price 6d:
Maclean, Printer, 9, Bow-street, London. VIVANT REX & REGINA

*Plate 6*

Program with Chapmans supporting Mrs. Siddons

*Plate 7*

Sam Drake Sr. in *King Lear*

*Plate 8 (below)*

John Philip Kemble in *Pizarro*

What worried him most was the hard-earned savings his father had invested in his schooling. But he was in love. No doubt of that. He was doubly in love. He was in love with Miss Fisher *and* the profession.

In a short time he had his theological degree. His parents had expected that he would become a curate and step into his father's living when that parent passed on. An easy course from one point of view but an impossible path for him to follow. The most difficult thing to be faced now that he knew his own mind was the telling of his parents. But he would not hold the truth in abeyance.

It took him six days to walk to Tidmouth and another half day to reach his home. Timidly, feeling like a stranger, he rapped gently on the worn door. It swung open and his mother, pale and wide-eyed, stood there in silence. They looked at each other for one uncomfortable moment; although he had been away for over two years, he still had a slight fear of his mother. Then, without a smile, she took him in her arms.

"How are you, Mother dear? And how is Father?"

She held him at arms' length and looked at him contentedly, apparently satisfied with what she saw. In continued silence, she pointed to a corner of the room. Her son's eyes followed the gesture. There in the faint light he made out a coffin. His mother spoke as he walked to it.

"Your father," she said, "died night before last."

Bryant looked at the old worn face, pitifully shrunken since last he saw him. He was not so old, not sixty. How different from the sprightly oldsters on the stage in London! He pitied the poor man and regretted the

95

sacrifices this parent had made. How his father had labored! Not enough food, not enough clothing; his whole life devoted to tending others and saving for his boy's education, the education he did not have in his youth.

*It were done. When 'tis done 'tis better it were done quickly.* It would have been sacrilege had his father known it, but he had heard those lines in the last play he had seen in London.

He took his mother's arm and walked with her into the back room.

"What now, Samuel?" she said, leading him now, as she always had, to face a situation with judgment.

He did not answer. How could he tell her?

"There's something on your mind, boy," she divined. "It worries you. Let me hear. I'm a Drake. We face things."

"I don't want to go into the Church, Mother," he said then.

"Not go into the Church?" she said softly. "What then, my boy?"

"It may sound strange and ungrateful to you, but I want to be an actor. After the way father. . . ."

He could go no further. A sigh, almost a groan, escaped him. But then, looking at his mother, he realized that it was not fear he felt; it was, rather, the force of her strength that overwhelmed him. Never consciously having needed it before, he had resented it in her. But now it was clear. She was a Drake, indeed, a great-grandniece of the Admiral. Never compromising like his father, never saying in difficulties that everything was "for the best."

"Why not be an actor?" she said. "Why not be anything but what your father was? Why spend your life struggling as he did, among these people who never appreciated or supported him properly? They will treat you the same way. Yes, be something else. But not here. Go to a *new* country, go to America. That's the place for a young man. This place has given out, like your father there."

The speech was filled with more concern and tenderness for his well-being than he had expected. He took her in his arms again, this time with deep feeling.

"But you, Mother? What of you?"

"I'll manage by myself," she said. "Your sisters are married and no longer a care. I'll follow you if I live long enough."

Bath was the place to start from. He could walk there. It had the only royal theater license in the West. Wealthy, retired people and the newly-rich merchants were attracted to the town because of its hot springs medicinal baths and exclusive society. Beau Brummell shined each night in the Pump Room; the courtesan and the gambler prospered; and top gaming houses were filled to capacity. A doorkeeper sat outside one of the plush money palaces in a huge hooded and winged chair. The chair turned aside the gusts of wind and the doorkeeper turned aside all but the proper entrants.

Colley Cibber, now a withered eighty, in red-heeled shoes and a great wig, ogled the pretty girls in the streets and cleared his throat audibly as they passed by. He was living the part he'd acted best—that of a fop. He'd had the voice and figure of a dandy, but they hissed his Iago and hooted his Richard off the stage. He'd been a cue-muffer and a puffer supreme.

Lorgnettes, fans, snuff, diamond-headed canes, enticing miss and coxcomb . . . all was elegance, show and sham.

This was Bath.

It was also the home of Miss Fisher and her family. The Fishers were great favorites of the Bath theater. The father was a silent and martial looking man, but Bryant liked him instinctively. Mr. Fisher, holding his own counsel was, unknown to Bryant, responsible for the latter securing the position of assistant stage manager at the Theatre Royal. Once behind the curtain his Oxford training became an advantage.

The management and the company liked and respected him. Of that he was certain. But he was *not* certain of Miss Fisher, at least, not enough to speak his mind to her. He had the dressing room next to hers and the girl who played the ladies' maid. He found himself eavesdropping on their small talk between the acts. They had a playful way of expressing their thoughts by quotations from plays. The number of lines these children of the theater had in their heads was astounding.

One night during an intermission, with one more act yet to go, he met her in the dark lane behind the backdrop. He hadn't said more than three words when her father called her. Another chance gone, he thought. When would he bring himself to address her again?

He went to his dressing room and sat down to wing his part through before ringing down the final curtain. There were voices in the next room. They distracted him and he stopped to listen. He heard his love say to her roommate:

I did not take my leave of him, but had
Most pretty things to say: Ere I could tell him
How I would think on him at certain hours,
Such thoughts and such. Or to have charged him
At the sixth hour of morn, at noon, at midnight
To encounter me with Orisons, for then
I am in Heaven with him; or ere I could
Give him that parting kiss which I had set
Betwixt two charming words, comes in my Father
And, like the tyrannous breathing of the north
Shakes all our buds from growing.

On this hint, Bryant, meeting her a moment later
coming out of her dressing room, gave and received the
kiss "betwixt two charming words." Much to his surprise,
her father seemed delighted with the ensuing romance.

They married and, as the years sped by raised a
family of four. With it all, Bryant had not lost the
vision his mother had given him of the new country,
but there was so much to interfere. Foremost, there was
a threat of war between the American colonies and
Mother England. Bryant sided with the colonies; he
would chance it with them. But there remained the
question of funds for the journey. With a family the
size of his he would need thirty pounds for the sea trip
alone. There was also his mother; he would have to
provide for her, but now he could thank his father for
leaving her the tiny house they had always lived in.

Sam visited her often and on one of these visits he
walked to the little stream where he had played as a
boy. There was a wool storage barn nearby which now
seemed strangely silent. Two men came from the
building, one of them a man Bryant knew, William
Tilbury, a merchant and the richest man in the shire.

99

Bryant and Tilbury greeted each other and, after bidding the other man adieu, they started to walk in the direction of town.

"Well, my boy," said Tilbury, "so now you're educated and married and back home, but still won't take your father's place."

"You think that is wrong of me, sir?" said Sam.

"On the contrary. That's good, I think. I was sorry to hear of the old man's going, but I never thought you would make a good pastor anyway."

"I never really wanted to be one," said Bryant. "I've had my mind set on other things."

"So. And what are your ambitions, boy?" asked the merchant.

"To remain an actor," said Bryant. "To have my own company. To perform in London, and one day perhaps, to go to America. I've had a small taste of it. Through my friends in the theater, Dick Sheridan and George Colman, I met the girl I married and by whom I have a family. She's still an actress, now playing at Drury Lane."

Tilbury walked beside the younger man in silence. When at last he spoke his voice was low and wistful.

"My boy," he said sighing, "no one hereabouts knows what I have to say. The people in this county only know that I'm rich, the richest man for miles around. But now that you've brought back memories, I'll tell you. In my youth I was once an actor. I traveled through county after county, through Wales, even through Scotland. At the fairs we played on a platform, out in the open, rain or shine. Ah, that was a wonderful, wonderful life! I've never regretted the years I spent at it. Sam," a brisk, businesslike ring entered his voice, "the wool business is in a slump. I've just closed that carding house we left. I'd like to try the theater again. What do we need?"

"Well, first," said Bryant, "we need plays."

"That's done," Tilbury replied. "I've kept them all— the ones we played at the fairs. They're the same today. No change in that for years. What next?"

"Places to play," said Bryant, "theaters."

"We can use my carding houses. I have seven empty at this moment, stretching from here to Chiddingold. They'll never be used for work again and there's enough lumber to make benches and a stage. We'll have a circuit. We'll play every town within a hundred miles. What next?"

"Actors."

"Pshaw!" said the merchant. "There's scores of strollers around. We can pick up a bushel basket of them between here and London in a week. Plays, theaters, actors. What else?"

"Well . . ." said Bryant, "there's money. To really start you need money."

"Now you've hit a tender spot, lad. I hate to spend money. That's how I became rich. I just hate to part with the stuff." He thought a moment. "But I have an idea. Sam Davis, the tailor who makes my clothes, has money. He wanted to invest in my business, but now as I have no business I'll tackle him on this. I think he'll like it. We'll each take a third. He's a clever, honest fellow. He'll handle the tickets and the orders. My boy, in good time we'll be thriving."

The theatrical circuit of Sam Bryant had begun. But his eyes were still on the new country.

The time finally came. He went to tell the grandniece of the Admiral. She was not surprised.

"Go," she said, "it's the place for a young man and his family. You can send for me later if you wish. Meanwhile, I'll manage by myself." She had not changed from the first time she had bid him go to the fledgling States.

"Mother," he said, "I'll send for you as soon as I can. And, your family name will live, for I'll take it. I'm Sam Drake of the theater in America from now on."

*Federal Street Theatre, Boston*

Chapter 7

# O Brave New World

Two strong influences combined to cause Will Chapman Sr. to forsake Covent Garden after thirty-five years and leave with his family, for the New World across the sea.

The first was a young and beautiful Irish actress who was engaged by the manager of the theater in 1805. Penelope Britt had been to America with her family in the formative period following the Revolutionary War and as a child had played at the famous John Street Theatre in New York. After her return home she became one of the most promising actresses on the Dublin stage, which led to her being booked by Mr. Harris of Covent Garden for an engagement in Liverpool; from there he brought her to London. She opened on the first day of November, 1805, as Moggy M'Gilpin in *Highland Reel*. Her talent and beauty was not wasted on Will Chapman. Within twelve months they were married. From Penelope, Will learned of the wonders and opportunities of the new land. She did not live to see it again, but she bore her husband a brood that was to cross the seas with him.

The second influence came from an American, John Howard Payne, a truly remarkable fellow. No one knows exactly when this precocious genius became stage-struck, but it is recorded that while working as a clerk, at the age of fifteen, he also edited and published a theatrical magazine of eight pages. Within a year after that he wrote a four-act play.

The magazine was a rehash of material that had been written many years before, an amateur's opinion of trends in the theater, followed by letters from correspondents, almost all of which were written by the editor himself. Under an assumed name he would write a blistering attack on a subject or personality and then indite a reply just as vehement with any signature other than his own. Many of the scenes in his play were taken boldly from already standard works.

At the age of eighteen Payne was an Apollo with a melodious voice. It was inevitable that a shrewd manager saw in him the making of an actor and attached himself to this wonder youth.

During his first season in America, along with minor classics, Payne "had himself up in" and played Hamlet, Romeo and Othello in all the theatrical centers along the

Atlantic coast. But Payne's acting, like many other things in his life, was all show and no insight, a poll-parrot series of readings accompanied by meaningless gestures. As a boy wonder he had been a novelty worth seeing. As a full-grown man his interpretations of Shakespeare could not please the groundlings and sorely grieved the judicious. Nor would he listen to his manager; with the receipts declining he cut loose from the man who had first promoted him and took the running of the company into his own hands. This was at the end of his third theatrical year and resulted in a plunge into debt from which he never fully recovered.

He had great charm and the faculty of making and keeping influential friends; it was at last through their bounty that a fund of two thousand dollars was collected to send him on a try of his luck in London. There are indications that fundamentally this was a scheme to be rid of him; it succeeded for a period of twenty years.

In the great English city he was warmly received as an actor, but this was soon over. The experienced British public soon recognized that there was no real depth to this handsome youth's acting; one season in the metropolis and another in the provinces was as long as he survived in the theater.

There followed two decades during which he became a hack playwright, served a term in jail for debt and was rewarded a few morsels of success.

He struck real fire once with *Brutus, the Fall of Tarquin*. The leading stars of England and America played in it for several seasons until the experts made public that many of the scenes were derived from eight different tragedies. It soon passed into oblivion.

Toward the end of his career in London, Payne tried his hand at several musical plays. For one of these he had induced the great English composer, Sir Henry Bishop, to write the tunes for his lyrics. Sir Henry became involved in the collaboration principally because of the talent of an Irish lass whose sister the year before had made her mark by singing Bishop's beautiful setting for the Shakespearean lyric, "Bid Me Discourse," while playing the part of the beauteous Olivia in *Twelfth Night*. Olivia has no songs in the original script, but Miss Tree had a voice, so they made a song out of some of the early lines of *Venus and Adonis* and added them to Olivia's first garden scene with Sebastian:

Bid me discourse, I will enchant thine ear,
Or, like a fairy, trip upon the green,
Or, like a nymph, with long and disheveled hair,
Dance on the sands, and yet no footing seen:
Love is a spirit all compact with fire,
Not gross to sink, but light, and will inspire.

When the young Irish beauty sang this, the London audience was won over. Her name was Ellen Tree and two years afterward her sister Maria was to become internationally famous as the wife of the Earl of Bolton.

After putting to music the songs of Shakespeare and other poets, Sir Henry could not be satisfied with the doggerel offered him by Payne. The whole thing was a nightmare to him, but the company had been engaged, the scenery built and painted, and the opening date set. There was also an obligation to Miss Ellen Tree who had sung his "Bid Me Discourse" the year before. He could not withdraw. There were further complications in store for him. There were only two good voices in the company for this new play, those of Will Chapman and Maria Tree; and in all the faulty rhymes Payne had offered him there was not one couplet that was suitable for Miss Tree.

Overnight John Howard created a new song for Maria, and early the next morning Sir Henry said he would do nothing with it. As usual, the lyrics were plagiarized, and clumsily at that. Bishop had other professional reasons for rejecting Payne's work; the phrases were too long, the vowels were in the wrong place, the words were dull and superficial.

Finally a simple musical theme was suggested that might fit the words. Whether it was something Payne had heard in France during one of his flights from creditors or whether Bishop discovered the tune in his library of folk songs has never been made clear; the air was note for note a repeat of a well-known, old-time French ballad. Two days before the opening Bishop walked into the rehearsal of *Clari, the Maid of Milan* with a lead sheet that would fit the words Payne had written. Sir Henry had been forced to go along with his partner in being a "snapper-upper of unconsidered trifles" and has gone down in history as the composer of the music.

Miss Maria Tree did her best, but the play had a respectable run of only twelve nights. On the program for the third night the modest announcement of the song was reprinted in a size equal to that of the title. On the sixth night it was featured above the play. By the time *Clari* closed, the song was being sung by everyone in London who could carry a tune. In a single year one hundred thousand copies were sold and the publishers made two thousand guineas. Payne received neither a single penny nor even a complimentary copy. His name was not in the billing on the program.

But Payne had to the end a faculty for making friends, and Will Chapman was one of them. Indeed, the Chapmans, and in later years the Drakes, were very close to him throughout his last years in the theater. Both families helped him all they could on both sides of the Atlantic.

After *Clari* closed, Payne was soon in dire straits again. His friends had to chip in anew to get him back home. New York gave him a rousing benefit. Edwin Forrest played Payne's *Brutus* that evening and Harry Chapman —Sam Chapman's son—appeared in one of his afterpieces. Payne's net was ten thousand dollars. His creditors got most of it. Then his friends secured a position for him as consul in far-off Algiers. It was there that he died at the age of sixty-one.

"Covent Garden" Chapman, after he came to this country, had one of his daughters sing the song from *Clari* in almost every comedy he played on his showboat, and his fiddler *played them out* with it every night. In those days "Home, Sweet Home"—for that was the title of the song—was sure-fire sentiment and sent the audience home singing and humming.

During his hard times in London, Payne had received a strong helping hand from the Drakes. Years later he tried to repay these favors by giving Mrs. Drake an effusive letter when she contemplated an invasion of London town in 1833. Introducing her to Daniel O'Connell, Esq., M.P., Irish leader of the time, Payne noted:

A lady of the highest standing both as a gentlewoman and an actress, Mrs. Drake of the Western region of our Western World, visits Europe and intends to make a professional experiment in London. I have thought I could greatly serve her and gratify you by making you known to each other; and as Mrs. Drake will probably visit Ireland I shall consider any attention she may receive through you as a compliment from you to our republic, as well as my countrymen.

And so it was that the fever of migrating to America touched the Chapmans too. The influences were many and strong. Young Will had sent back glowing reports to his family which, along with Penelope's many praises before she died, and the words of Payne set them to thinking.

A family conclave was held. William Sr., George, Sam, Elizabeth and Sarah each aired their private views on what course their future should take. They found, happily enough, that they were in unanimous agreement: America was the place to go. They put their plan into action at once. There were theatrical commitments to be fulfilled, passages to be arranged and packing to be done. It took some time, but at length they set sail for New York taking with them Caroline, the offspring of young Will, and little Harry—Sam Chapman's son. Shortly after their arrival, the Chapmans were firmly established on the American stage.

The principal theaters were then on Chambers Street and the Bowery; Broadway was not as sophisticated an area as it is today. The gas street lights were rarely lit and through the darkened street the enormous canine population of the city roamed, hungry and continually on the prowl. Hardly an hour went by in which fire wagons did not rush down the streets.

Between engagements in the big city the Chapmans, having an affection for "the road," played Albany, Troy, Trenton, Wilmington and Philadelphia.

The Quaker City immediately claimed Sam and he settled there as co-manager of the Walnut Street Theatre. The Walnut, one of the most historical playhouses on the Atlantic seaboard, opens its doors to patrons of the drama to this day.

When Sam came to the Walnut its boards were held by a resident company. Among the regulars of the cast was the favorite actress of the town, the young and beautiful Elizabeth Jefferson. She was an aunt of Joseph Jefferson of later *Rip Van Winkle* fame. In fact, Sam was a Rip before Jefferson, the part having been one of those he played in Philadelphia.

There was a mystery about Sam. He had two young children with him, Harry and Caroline, but no wife. Most people assumed that he was a widower, but some could not resist speculating that perhaps his wife had eloped with a nobleman or that the children were illegitimate.

In spite of this, Sam soon proved himself a worthy fellow with such tact and talent in his favor that, in the very first weeks of his engagement, he won the admiration of the town and the love of the fair Elizabeth. This seemingly perfect match was wrecked with tragic suddenness, however, leaving Elizabeth a young widow with an unborn child.

The indirect cause of Sam's death was the holdup of the Reading Mail.

The Reading Mail, with four fine, fast horses, carry-

ing nine male passengers and the driver, was stopped
by three highwaymen, Porter, Potete and Wilson, a few
miles from Philadelphia in the vicinity of a city now
called Germantown.

The horses were unhitched and fastened to the fence,
and the driver's and passengers' hands were tied behind
them with their own handkerchiefs. Porter, an Irishman,
seemed to be in command and was reported by the victims to be extremely well-mannered. When one victim
said his watch was a present from his sweetheart, it was
returned by Porter with a princely bow; and when he
found an untouched plug of tobacco in a pocket he took
a *chaw* and returned the package to its owner. He divided the loose change equally among the captives so
that they might breakfast and return home in health.
He conducted the whole affair with admirable decorum
and took such respectful leave of his victims that the
reports made him paradoxically a hero.

But the theft of mail bags involved the U.S. government in the chase. The men were caught in about ten days
and rushed to trial. President Jackson spared Wilson,
who was young and whose father had been a soldier
under "Old Hickory"; Potete had turned state's evidence;
but Porter, whose urbanity had won the admiration of
everyone, was hanged for this most gentlemanly piece
of highwayism.

Chapman, nicknamed "Fighting Sam," was known for
his dramatization of local incidents. This occurrence had
caused much excitement and Sam saw in it his chance
for a full-length play.

First he visited the scene of the robbery to localize the
action of his work. He went over the ground carefully

and made sketches. In remounting his horse, the animal shied and Sam slightly barked the skin on one of his shoulders. That night on the stage he had to wear a suit of brass armor, and, the weather being excessively hot, he wore it next to his skin. The shoulder scratch became infected and Sam died within a week.

It was the custom in the City of Brotherly Love for a vast number of people to attend funerals, whether or not they knew or had ever heard of the deceased. Because Chapman had been so popular, his death so unexpected, and his wife adored by everyone, there was a huge concourse.

Joe Cowell, a colleague of the Chapmans but one who could not successfully compete with them theatrically, walked with two prominent men whose influence he expected to use in a prospective engagement. Cowell was absorbed in listening to figures and boasting of former triumphs when another procession cut through his group, going in a different direction and causing some confusion.

When the crowd reached the cemetery, Cowell proposed that the trio move toward the grave so as to make the Chapman family aware of their attendance. They did so and listened with special reverence to the beautiful service.

Then they looked around with the timid glance always assumed on such occasions, but no look of recognition was exchanged. They peeped less guardedly from under their handkerchiefs and took careful note of each weeping mourner. There was no old William Chapman, no handsome young William, no George, neither of the two girls. All were strangers.

The truth dawned upon them. They had gotten mixed up in the other procession, led to the wrong graveyard and moved to tears over the wrong corpse.

Some citizens of Philadelphia, more sincere than Cowell, erected a modest marble monument to Sam Chapman in a cemetery since converted into a playground in a slum section of the city. These admirers covered much ground in the inscription on his monument. It read as follows:

> To Their Favorite Comedian
> By the Citizens of Philadelphia
> His Friends Adored Him
> Even His Enemies Loved Him

His theatrical descendants passing through in engagements saw that the mound was well kept and the lettering made clear throughout the years. But the neighborhood slowly declined from its original respectability.

His great-grandson, one hundred and eighteen years later, was the last to make a visit. He found that Sam's monument had been overturned by hoodlums, the marble blocks scattered about and tar poured over the inscription. In addition, many graves had been opened and the bones placed in cartons. The lady who kept the cemetery related that in Sam's grave there had been a receptacle containing a bundle of papers. They were so water soaked, she said, that she had thrown them away!

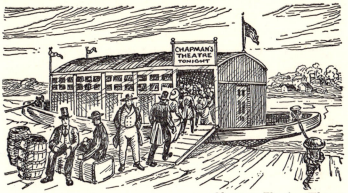

*Chapman Floating Theatre*

## Chapter *8*

# Here Comes the Showboat

With the untimely passing of Sam Chapman in Philadelphia, old William was determined more than ever to hold his family together. It could not be done by playing the theaters in New York with occasional scattered trips outside the state. Something more profitable, on the one hand, and more economical, on the other, was needed.

An engagement in Pittsburgh gave him the idea. He noted that a tremendous river traffic had come to life, with a thousand craft trading up and down the stream. After a play date in Louisville and one in Cincinnati, his mind was made up.

He would buy a large boat and transform it into a theater. The family would live there by day and act on it by night.

It was quite an innovation and inspired many legends about the Chapmans and their way of life. They were gypsies, it was said, speaking among themselves a strange tongue. As a matter of fact, they were the products of the finest years of the English-speaking stage and the jargon they used as a joke on the natives of the then Far West was a mixture of Cockney and improvised French they had picked up as youngsters.

Originally, the Chapmans' river boat, christened *The Theatre*, was to be a seasonable occupation. During the warm months the family troupe would play the river towns and during the regular theatrical season perform in the established centers. But the "playhouse on a raft," forerunner of the elegant showboat, proved so successful that it took the full year to complete the tour.

*The Theatre* was built in Pittsburgh of the best oak and white pine that could be found. It was launched on the beautiful Ohio and floated past hills and through enchantingly rural valleys, the foliage along the banks brilliant eight months of the year. Today, logging, erosion, refuse and acids from factories have changed all that. But in the era before the ruination, during the ten years that the Chapmans sailed the great rivers of interior America, the lucent aquamarine waters of the Ohio surpassed any of the lovely streams of old England. *The Theatre* sometimes moored during the day at places that seemed like unexplored wildernesses, but once the news that "The players have come!" had mysteriously spread, by nightfall, guided by the candles in the windows of the craft, people found their way there on foot, horseback, and by wagon. The floating theater not only brought enjoyment to many cities and settlements, it also provided shelter and a means of existence for the players. Life on the showboat was pleasant for its occupants, as well as profitable.

Payment to see the play was in barter—chickens, fruit, vegetables, cured meats or a few yards of cloth. Money was welcome, of course, but the Chapmans had a box office policy that survives to this day; they took what the people had. The Virginia Barter Theatre is the closest twentieth century example of this unique system.

But the system had its drawbacks. One night the audience seemed to outnumber the receipts. The eldest daughter was at the *gate* and dropped the take into a box behind her. A young boy had paid with a dressed chicken which he retrieved from the box and passed back to the dock to be used again. Chapman Sr. finally figured it out and estimated that about eighty percent of the audience was seeing the play for nothing. He untied the vessel and let her slip downstream about four miles before tying her up again. Everyone, honest people as well as cheats, had to walk back to the landing.

The Chapmans were born fishermen, as well as actors, expert at dropping a line at any hour of the day or night. The problem was how to combine angling with acting.

Like all comedians, George Chapman wanted to play roles least suited to his talents. As often as he could he enacted heavy, tragic, stage villains. One evening he had worked himself into the mood for Iago and was waiting for his entrance.

He had been fishing all afternoon without any luck, but he was certain that the next tug on the line would

mean a catch. He called to a young helper to hold the
line for him while he put a few last-minute touches to
his make-up. Then, just before his entrance cue, he went
to check on his linesman. The unreliable boy was gone,
so George tied the line to his ankle and went on stage.

Although Othello tripped over the line once in the
early moments of the scene, all was going well until
George's leg came out from under him like a shot and
sent him sprawling on the boards. He recovered with a
speech never written by the Bard:

"My lord," he said, "in my great love for you I have
gone too far. I will leave you one moment to your
thoughts. Anon I will return."

Off he went to retrieve his catch while Othello, his
face hidden in his hands to suppress laughter as much as
to suggest thought, waited for Iago to haul in his fish.

But after pulling with all his might, the monster cat-
fish "cut" and suddenly changed his tactics. He jumped
out of the water and landed in the boat. The sudden
slackening took Iago so completely by surprise that he
staggered back on his heels and onto the stage, dragging
the fifty-pound catch after him.

They played the performance to the end, but after his
first scene Iago's villainy didn't seem to mean much to the
plot.

But despite such blunders and other mishaps occa-
sioned by sudden changes in the weather, Old Chapman's
idea was successful. To eliminate competition and live
more comfortably, the next obvious step was the purchase of a larger, more impressive "house." The only
way to obtain this was by raising the admission fee. The
regular theaters on land were charging as high as seventy-

five cents per seat; the Chapmans had already come up from a nickel to a quarter in cash or barter. Now they decided to make the admission charge fifty cents. In one instance, however, the public retaliated.

While the night's performance was in progress, someone who did not have the extra twenty-five cents cut the boat from its moorings. It began to glide downstream with the tide, but so intent were the actors and the audience with the unfolding of the play that they were unaware of participating themselves in an unscheduled drama. Indeed, it wasn't until the boat struck the bank with a sudden shock three miles down the river that they had the slightest intimation they were adrift.

However, the receipts were so satisfactory that the Chapmans decided to tie up right where they were and open the following evening with a new program. The audience was so pleased with the entertainment that they took the walk back home in high spirits and promised to return the next night for the change in bill.

But on another occasion the vessel was slipped from her moorings with serious consequences. *The Theatre* had docked at the newly-formed "Young Woman's Settlement."

This community had not existed when the Chapmans' modern ark floated down the river the previous season. This was not unusual, for as America expanded westward new towns sprang up like mushrooms. These communities resembled each other closely; unless there was some distinguishing feature, a stranger might easily think he was in Young Woman's Settlement, for instance, when actually he was in another town with a name as equally quaint.

Young Woman's had made itself a harbor, of course, and Old Will was quick to pick himself the best moorings before any other craft also decided to tie in. Once moored, the board planks were set up leading from boat to land and the usual campaign for patronage began.

Banners were hoisted in the breeze, drums were beat and trumpets blown: ancient fanfare to announce the important event. And indeed it was an occasion, for the entire community turned out in force; anyone who could walk came to watch or help *The Theatre* dock.

After the instruments had achieved their effect, Old Will, as captain, took charge of the situation. He delivered a truly compelling word picture of the wonders in store and then introduced the members of the cast, each with an appropriate blast from the trumpet. Finally he urged the bedazzled onlookers to step right up and put it across the board for the ticket of admission that would insure their having a choice seat at the performance.

He told the good citizens of Young Woman's that money was not important, that tickets could be had in exchange for produce of the area—a goose or a dressed chicken, a side or a leg of meat, a bottle of wine or rum, a share of eggs, potatoes, pumpkins or pawpaws, apples or corn. The quantity of each varied according to where the purchaser wished to sit—in the boxes, the pit, or the gallery.

The response was tremendous. The divertissement-starved denizens of Young Woman's bought as many seats as the vessel could accommodate. The performance was to be given the next night.

*The Theatre*'s crew was heartened to the point of exhilaration. Old Chapman ordered a celebration in honor

of the generous and discerning populace of Young
Woman's and intoned, almost as a benediction, the fer-
vent wish that their prosperity and numbers increase.
There was much hilarity on land and on board; especially
on board where the bowls of rum punch were more
numerous and potent than even this occasion required.

At last the male members of the seagoing temple of
Thespis lay, or slid, down to sleep. With or without their
blankets, they had a good sleep, a very good sleep, one
of the soundest of their lives.

The libations on land had aftereffects as well. Most
took it in their stride, but some, notably the younger
rowdies, were incited to the pitch of a first-class spree.
Since the presence of *The Theatre* had induced their
state of alcoholic exuberance, *The Theatre* was also the
butt of their pranks. They managed to keep quiet long
enough to steal down to the harbor around midnight and
cut loose the craft from its moorings.

So silently had the operation been performed that not
one of the cast or crew awoke. In blissful ignorance they
drifted gently with the smooth current without a lurch
or a bump to disturb them.

That is, until several hours and twenty miles later,
when, at six in the morning, they were more than rudely
awakened by an abrupt meeting with the pier-head of
Uncle Sam's Town, as new and raw in appearance as its
neighbor upstream.

Shocked at that moment into wakefulness, Old Chapman was none the less sure of what happened. He sprang
to his feet and onto deck with the order, "All hands
ahoy! Wake there, you slumbering angels! We have
come unfast of our moorings. Make taut our lines!"

The inhabitants of Uncle Sam's Town were surprised to find that *The Theatre*, already bedecked, had slipped in upon them during the night. But they were not unhappy about it. It was a grand event for which the entire community turned out; old and young, barber and farmer, bachelor and widow, miller and jailer, all flocked to the harbor with cries and shouts of elation.

Old Will saw them coming and drew back in alarm.

"Wait!" he cried. True, he had prayed for the increase and prosperity of Young Woman's Settlement, but he hadn't expected it to be granted overnight! "Not another ticket can be sold!" he shouted to the bewildered pleasure seekers. "Not another one, I tell you! Every seat has already been engaged. The vessel positively will not hold another person and we can not stay over another night. We must beat the island freshets to New Orleans. Please, inform your friends and neighbors that only those now holding tickets can be accommodated. I'm very sorry, but I'm sure you understand."

While the crew took the day to recover from their hang-over, the residents of Uncle Sam's Town met to discuss the queer behavior of theater folks. It was a severe disappointment, to be sure, for they might have to wait a whole year for another appearance. Enquiries were made throughout the town but the inhabitants could not find anyone who held a ticket for admission. There was just no accounting for the strange actions of some *outsiders*.

As the soft evening came on, the lamps on the boat were lit; the time of the performance was at hand and the actors were all dressed and waiting. The quadrille band played the overture and Old Will stood ready to greet the ticket holders and spread his usual good will.

The hour, the minute, arrived and passed. No one came on board, although the river bank was covered with people watching for Will's audience.

The overture blared out again, and for a third time. The inhabitants of Uncle Sam's Town could stand it no longer. There on the river bank they began to nudge each other, stamp their feet and approach a high state of merriment.

"Blast them!" Will exploded. "If they want to load us up with commodities and cash and then stand out there grinning like jackanapes—well, let 'em! We're going downstream."

Varying fortunes rewarded their efforts, but mostly the season was prosperous. They had given many afternoon as well as evening performances, and the troupe arrived at New Orleans with a respectable amount of money. Their storeroom was still well-packed and they added to their profits by selling the surplus goods to the markets of the Crescent City. *The Theatre* and flatboat which now accompanied it were dismantled, the wood sold for lumber, and a final accounting made.

The Chapman coffers were indeed abundant and so they disdained to use the overland trail back to Pittsburgh this time. They decided to take a steamer to New York, where they would fill their time with whatever engagements might be secured until spring came again.

The following year they made their way to the "Birmingham of America," Pittsburgh, where they constructed their new theater and set out upon the water. A new season had been christened.

Late one evening they docked at the pier-head of Young Woman's Settlement. They retired and slept well, if not as soundly as the last time they had been at this port.

The following morning the well-known procedure took place. The town assembled en masse, Old Will made his speech, introduced the members of the cast and described the glories of the bill to be presented. Although his announcement was not met with enthusiasm, almost every ticket was sold, but not for food. Every admission was paid for in cash! But the larder was full, so all cash was not displeasing. It was singular behavior for this part of the country, but Old Will had learned to take his good fortunes when and where he found them with no questions asked.

Evening came on. The boat lamps were lit and the door thrown open. The boxes, the benches of the pit and gallery were soon filled to overflowing. It was a waiting, purposeful assemblage, and Will sensed something foreboding about the atmosphere. But he was sure that it would disappear as soon as the gay proceedings began.

The band struck up an overture based on nautical and patriotic airs, including *America,* for which the words had recently been composed. It was not greeted with huzzas; the audience "sat on its hands."

Up went the curtain to reveal the entire cast dressed in their most impressive costumes, smiling their warmest smiles, and ready to give their best. No welcoming applause greeted them. It was a warm evening, and the only sound from the audience was that of the fans that fluttered like butterflies in the hands of the ladies.

Old Will, the most resplendently costumed of all the males, stepped forward and made his bow to the house. The silence was disconcerting, but he dutifully gave the signal for the lovely opening bars of the introductory chorus.

The audience awoke. The harmony of the actors' voices was drowned in a thundering cacophony of hisses and unsavory epithets. Not only that, the performers, whose intention had been to please, were besieged with a well-aimed shower of ripe eggs, overripe tomatoes and boiled potatoes. The cast hastily retreated to safer quarters, some even preferring to take to the hold.

Will alone held his ground amid the startling cries of "Serpent!" "Scoundrel!" "Tar and feathers!" He begged them to state their reasons for the attack. He soon learned.

"You remember this place from last year, don't you? We remember you, you poor excuse for an honest man! We brought you our fowl, our vegetables, our best quarters of lamb. And you cast off in the dead of night! Well, you can cut off and run again. And *you'd better*—as soon as we're willing to let you."

A glimmer of the true circumstances slowly came to Chapman's mind. It wasn't entirely clear yet, but he had a vague notion that this reception was somehow tied in with a highly profitable nonperformance of last season, a rare event not easily forgotten.

He was eager to make amends—a free performance, even two free performances—but the citizens of Young Woman's Settlement were in no mood for reparations. They shouted him down and subjected him to a new torrent of flying objects. Old Chapman was forced to make an ignoble retreat, the curtain was quickly lowered to protect him and the resulting cheers from the angry crowd were greater than if the performance had been given.

On making their noisy way back to land, the crowd wreaked considerable damage to the trappings and embellishments of the vessel, as well as to the boat itself. Chapman did not linger for repairs. He gave orders to cast off immediately, and balefully awaited the running of the tide.

The following night they treated the joyous citizens of Uncle Sam's Town to the performance so unconsciously denied them the year before.

But their days of idly drifting down the river were numbered. Steam was the order of the day. Since Fulton's contribution to progress in 1798, steam had come into favor so fast that when one wanted to indicate that anything, from babies to actors, were being turned out too quickly they simply said the product was made by steam.

The times, in truth, were changing; speed and profit were essential, and the Chapmans were not blind to the usefulness of the new discovery. With this new aid to navigation, the trips between stands could be of greater length so that only the substantial and fastest growing settlements need be played. In addition, the trip upstream could be made by boat, avoiding the long, dangerous jaunt by horseback with one lone wagon for the costumes and wigs.

The journey downstream was profitable again and the scrapping of *The Theatre* brought a sizeable return. The Chapmans were able to buy five horses and a wagon

Plate 9

Charles D. Rice,
originator of the minstrel act

Plate 10

Alexander Drake as a comic singer

Plate 12

George Frederick Cooke in *Richard III*

# PROVIDENCE THEATRE

THE managers have the pleasure of announcing to the publick that they have engaged

## MR. COOKE

To perform in the Providence Theatre for six nights only. During the engagement no play can be repeated.

In order to prevent difficulty, and give an equal chance to the publick in general to witness the brilliant performances of this justly celebrated actor, a box plan with the whole of the boxes regularly numbered will be opened at the Box Office of the Theatre, at ten o'clock on each day of performance, when places may be taken in any number not exceeding ten, nor less than two.

*This Evening*, July 13th, (1812,) will be presented for the only time this season, Shakspeare's celebrated comedy in five acts, called

## THE MERCHANT OF VENICE.

Shylock, (for that night only.) - - - Mr. Cooke.
of the Theatre Royal, Covent Garden, London, (his first appearance here.)

| Antonio, | - | - | - | - | - | Mr. Drake. |
| Gratiano, | - | - | - | - | Mr. Waring. |
| Bassanio, | - | - | - | - | Mr. Young. |
| Lorenzo, | - | - | - | - | Mr. Robertson. |
| Duke, | - | - | - | - | Mr. Clarke. |
| Launcelot, | - | - | - | - | Mr. Dickenson. |
| Gobbo, | - | - | - | - | Mr. Barnes. |
| Salanio, | - | - | - | - | Mr. Roberts. |
| Salarino, | - | - | - | - | Mr. Spiller. |
| Tubal, - | - | - | - | - | Mr. Entwistle. |
| Balthazar, | - | - | - | - | Master A. Drake. |
| Portia, | - | - | - | - | Mrs. Powell. |
| Nerissa, | - | - | - | - | Mrs. Young. |
| Jessica, (her first appearance in Providence,) | - | Miss Dellinger. |

Plate 11

Program with George Frederick Cooke and the Drakes

with enough left over to build a larger, more permanent boat for the next season.

They headed East in high spirits.

On their return by land, they had to pass through unsettled country with only a sprinkling of small communities and isolated log cabins along the way. The Chapmans were adept at dialects and quickly caught the speech patterns of the regions through which they passed. Their traveling clothes were homespun and their speech inflected in a manner quite different from the Covent Garden accent of their bringing-up. It was natural for them to try and fit into any situation or locality, yet strange were the characters at times encountered.

They had reached an Indian village. Indians were still a menace, if aroused, for the "Five Civilized Tribes" still held rights to eighteen million acres in the South.

The Chapmans passed through the village at a leisurely pace, and as they did so they saw a noted London actor of days gone by slinking from their wondering gaze into the shelter of an Indian cabin. The cabin was owned by the tribal chief, who had engaged him for a mere pittance to teach his children English. Circumstances or the desire to hide from life had made him go native to such a degree that he was a stranger to almost anyone who had known him in the days of his London prosperity. He would have escaped recognition this time as well had it not been for Old Will's keen eyes, which rarely forgot a face.

But his was not a singular case. Many refugees from the East were likewise hiding in the wilderness. All were not passive and retiring; some were dangerous to an extreme, which contributed to the frightening as well as uncomfortable aspects of a journey over the deeply rutted land. Highwayism of the most vicious brand was common. Mere robbery was not enough. Hapless travelers were frequently slaughtered, their bodies cut open, filled with stones and thrown into the streams. Therefore, it was inevitable that the Chapmans have a bout with a company of these outlaws sooner or later.

It happened when they were three weeks out of New Orleans. They were making their way slowly and were about to strike camp at dusk when they saw six horsemen approaching. They were the most ferocious looking cast of characters the family had ever seen, on stage or off. The Chapmans watched for the warning signs of an attack. If the party passed them all together on the right, all was well; but if the riders separated and passed them alternately on either side, one by one, they were most likely maneuvering for a holdup.

And now, sure enough, one rider passed to the right of the Chapman cavalcade and another passed to the left. The next pair did likewise. These four joined forces at the rear while the two remaining horsemen blocked the road and waited for the Chapmans to come to them. As if, under the circumstances, there was any other way for them to go!

"We're the Skeltons!" said one of the head men. By his slightly less outlandish dress he appeared to be the leader. His voice was loud, raucous and designed to intimidate.

"WE ARE THE CHAPMANS!" roared back George Chapman in a voice twice as loud and terrifying.

This seemed to take their accoster somewhat aback. He looked at his partner, who shook his head, denying recognition of the name. The leader looked back to George. His next speech was not quite so booming and more to the point.

"Who are you," he wanted to know, "and where are you bound for?"

"We're actors," came back the reply, "returning from a hard season in the South."

"Actors!" yelled the bandit to his henchmen in the rear. "Boys, we got actors! Not wax ones, but real flesh an' blood. They're alive, by Gawd!"

"If alive we be," retorted George, "it's only because we feed on things of the mind while our bellies are starving. We are, after the hard season just referred to, poor people trying to make our way back to home and friends."

"A likely story!" snapped the leader. "If you're so poor, how do you expect to make your 'way back to home and friends'?"

"How? indeed! I have already said that we're actors. We play for our lodging and sing for our suppers," said George.

"Hell!" roared the leader, slapping his thigh in sarcastic merriment. "Hitch up your horses, tie your wagon this side of the road and git ye all under that big tree by the clearin'. Come on up here, boys. We'll see what these actors can do."

When the *audience* and performers had taken their positions, the leader clapped his hands as a command and shouted, "We've eaten, now let us be entertained! And," he added significantly, "it had better be good!"

On a clearing to one side of the deserted road began an entertainment in which the actors had more than their reputations at stake. Old Will did the curse scenes from *King Lear* and *Julius Caesar*, and the soliloquies from *The Merchant of Venice* and *Richard III*. He continued, aided by his family, with the uproarious scenes from *Speed the Plough*. George and young Will sang comic songs and Caroline danced to Harry's fiddling, like an elf in the forest of Arden.

The performance ended with the Chapmans in line taking their customary bows while the robbers applauded and roared with laughter.

So far, so good, but the bandit leader, somewhat apologetically, said he would have to look through the wagon as a precaution and to satisfy his band. Whereupon he shook out the costumes, regarding them with wonder and taking great interest in the few tricky hand props and wigs. He found nothing of value to seize.

Finally he came to a box that had been used in the casket scene from *The Merchant of Venice*. He was about to open it when Caroline rushed up, crying, "No! No! You must not! You must not!" and fell sobbing into Will's arms.

"Brother," said George, "in there is the remains of this poor gal's child. Her husband skipped and the baby died the second day after birth. We're taking it back to rest with its ancestors in Pittsburgh."

The robber released his hold upon the box and there was a suspicion of tears in his eyes as he removed his hat and bowed. Upon returning his hat to his head he called to his companions to mount their steeds. They swung into saddle, and with shouts suitable for brigands, galloped on toward the west. The Chapmans, as soon as they readied their horses and wagon, raced with all possible speed in the opposite direction. It was late that night before they dared pitch camp again.

Their composure and split-second improvisation had not only saved their lives, but also their earnings. For the true contents of the alleged babe's coffin was the gold with which they intended to buy their new boat, the one to be powered by steam.

*The Theater moved West*

Chapter *9*

# Then Westward Ho!

When the Drakes found their way to Albany in 1814, it was a growing town with a population of about 10,000. The residences along the river were built in the old Dutch style. On State Street were a few mansions of the very rich. Old General Van Rennselaer and other members of the founding Dutch families were still elected as rulers of the community. The city had a geographical advantage, especially for trade; it was the turning point for one of the main routes to the great West.

The Albany Inn at 30 Eagle Street also became known as Mrs. Denny's inn. Captain John Denny died at sea on a trip to Killarney to visit his relatives, leaving his widow a house in Schenectady and five children. He had never applied for a pension.

The eldest Denny daughter, who had married Mr. Whitney, a prosperous storekeeper in Albany, urged her mother to sell her home and come over to the capitol city. Mrs. Denny, of old Holland stock, held out against any move that might mean loss of independence, so the keen Albany son-in-law traded her Schenectady property for the inn. West of the inn, where the capitol now stands, was the city's common, and Mrs. Denny pastured her cow there.

Albany had the legislature and a monied population, and there was a yearning for culture. Two blocks down the hill from Mrs. Denny's inn stood the Green Street Theatre which played to a more sophisticated audience than in earlier years. News traveled quickly. The theatergoer was aware of both the London and American reputations of their performers. Plays and players were talked about at parties and dinners, at the mansions and the inn.

When the owner of the theater casually mentioned that Mr. Bernard was coming to manage the house for a season, everyone knew, or soon found out, that Mr. Bernard the year before had managed the Federal Street Theatre in Boston, which was as fine a theatrical recommendation as one could have. Bernard had formerly been a successful London comedian and president of the *Beefsteak Club*, whose meetings equalled in wit and brilliance the Mermaid gatherings where Will Shakespeare and Ben Jonson had had their happy bouts. Bernard was bringing the most distinguished members of the Boston Company with him, and chief among his principals was Sam Drake, the stage manager.

The Drakes were the first to arrive in Albany for the new season. They put up at Mrs. Denny's inn and made arrangements to house the others of the company there as well. Mrs. Denny was glad to have them. They livened up the place and helped business at the bars. People came from Schenectady, twenty miles away, just to look at the actors. Through Mrs. Whitney, the eldest daughter, Drake met the elite of the town and took their orders for the season, and young Sam made a place for himself and the company with the members of the sporting circle. When Mr. Bernard arrived, his reception would have led one to suppose that he was a hero of the late war and not a subject of King George III, a very recent enemy.

Word soon got about that rehearsals were being held. The doors of the theater had to be locked and the windows boarded up against the curious.

Young Alexander Drake had become friendly with Frances Ann Denny and she was an exception to the rule that visitors be kept away from rehearsals. To her, the watching of a play taking shape was an exciting experience. She was just out of finishing school where she had been one of the pupils to mount the platform and best recite the Progress of Mr. Bunyan's *Pilgrim*.

Before the first week was over, young Alex had maneuvered an audition for her with his father. Sam was so pleased with the results that he promised to ask Mr. Bernard whether he might use her as one of Olivia's women in *Twelfth Night*. Mr. Bernard was too busy to hear the young lady, but Drake did not forget the promise she'd shown. Nor did Alex.

The theater was built of brick and seated about eight hundred people. It was in the very center of the town and served its purpose until 1880.

Drake found the stage adequate, with enough scenery stacked against the wall to equip any of the light comedies that Mr. Bernard had on his schedule. But he was not satisfied with the lighting. The candles were tallow and the drippings had caused much complaint. Therefore, he ordered sperm oil from New York and himself made a mold. He was quite adept at fashioning improvements for a theater; the new light was a success, it burned down to the cup without the loss of a drop.

There was one newspaper in Albany, and all that was printed was a politely worded card that Mr. Bernard was honored to announce to the ladies and gentlemen of Albany that his season would begin October 1st and their patronage was solicited.

The opening was a gala occasion. Governor Clinton sat in a box. Frances Ann stood in the wings.

The play season was inaugurated. It was well-attended, and the programs were varied.

In all, the Drakes spent a year living at the inn on Eagle Street, which stood until the spot was made into a parking lot in March of 1950.

One day in 1815 John Usher, a nephew of an old theatrical friend of Sam Drake, arrived in Albany with wonderful tales of the *new* country over the mountains. Kentucky, it was called, and settlers were traveling there by the thousands, many from old Virginia, bringing with them the solid money of that state.

John's uncle owned a sizeable piece of property in Lexington, the largest city of Kentucky at that time. Lexington's only theater was a converted salt house which was used by amateurs. Although their efforts were sincere and people were interested in the project, the entertainment itself was inadequate, and the house was not particularly adapted to the purpose it served. And so the nephew carried a message from his uncle to Drake: Luke Usher urged Sam to come to the new country and show what English professionals could do.

So the trip was planned. They would start in wagons and play at inns through the State of New York into Pennsylvania, down the Susquehanna River by boat, to an important frontier town called Pittsburgh. There they would buy a "longhorn," a sort of cabin on a raft steered by one long oar from the stern—the largest boat of this kind—and float down the Ohio River to Limestone, Kentucky. The journey by water over, they would sell the boat, buy horses and wagons and travel down the Limestone road to Lexington.

Sam Drake requested Mrs. Denny three times to allow Frances Ann to go in his care. Mrs. Denny knew the way of the people of the world, and although she respected the Drakes she hesitated to give her consent. It was not until the wagons were packed and ready to start that she could be prevailed upon.

Drake Sr. was the active leader of the troupe. He was called "The Old Gentleman," although he could not have earned the title with years. He lived on fully forty years as a prominent Kentucky figure. The company consisted of the Drake family, Frances Ann, four unrelated show folks and a youngster, N. M. Ludlow, who afterward wrote a famous book on the early theater in the Middle West. Sam Drake, who set out on the venture solely because of Usher's enthusiasm—show folks are notorious in that respect—had his own misgivings about the whole proposition. But the youngsters thought it a most delightful adventure. They were not wrong; in fact, the exodus from Albany to the Far West was probably the most singular in the annals of the American stage.

There were many wolf and Indian scares along the way to Pittsburgh, but no one was injured and it was exciting. En route they played only comedies, at which they were most adept. Almost no scenery was needed. They put up a curtain, borrowed chairs and let the word get about that there were actors at the inn and that a performance would be given. The admission fee was lodging for man and beast and fifty cents for each chair at the performance. The money taken was divided equally among the members of the company.

Spirits were continually high and Drake Sr. kept them at that level by telling the young ones stories of the good old days of the theater.

When the troupe reached Pittsburgh they found it a rather dismal town, blackened with coal dust and blanketed continually by smoke and cinders. Cheering, though, was the fact that there were many more people to bring to a performance than any place they had seen since Albany. The Old Gentleman's sensitive feel for real money responded immediately and he decided to forget the comedies and give them a straight, unadulterated tragedy. He had one in his box left over from the London stage, a tale of the conquest of Peru. In later days it would have been known as a hot subject.

*Pizarro* or *The Death of Peruvian Rolla* it was called. It required a full production, and Drake was equal to that. He bought canvas and, single-handed, painted stage drops for the scenes of a Temple of the Sun, the Throne of the Court of Pizarro, and the Bridge Scene for the famous escape with the child.

But a difficulty presented itself. There was a shortage of virgins. Virgins—stage virgins—were not to be had in Pittsburgh in those days. There was no wild scramble to get behind the footlights as there is today. Seamstresses and show-binders would sooner have thought of walking deliberately into Pandemonium than to have appeared on the stage as "supers." What was the use of a Temple of the Sun without Virgins of the Sun as worshippers? And without worshippers what would become of that beautiful chant, "Oh, Power Supreme! in mercy smile." No, there *must* be virgins; but how to get them? The local property man was assigned to overcome the difficulty.

In about two weeks, on a Saturday night early in September, the work was produced.

The house was filled to capacity. There were four hundred persons on hand, at a dollar a ticket each, except for children. The pit was crowded with foundrymen, keelboat men, and dark-featured and iron-fisted burghers. The boxes were filled with beautifully gowned women.

The curtain bell was rung promptly on time and up went the curtain, displaying to the eyes of the astonished little boys in the audience a magnificent tent scene—by Drake, naturally—the material very much like our modern striped street awnings, but looking more like a fine silk than canvas.

The tent was guarded by six *Spanish* soldiers in full armor of leather and buttons. The costumes did not exactly fit the soldiers, who were merely half-grown lads; the helmets were too large and slipped over their eyes. This was a convenience to the lads, who were most likely ashamed of being seen in such company. It was all right at rehearsals, but now, in front of their friends and townsmen—well! The leather armor, too, needed filling out, having been made for full-sized men, and on the backs of the boys frozen there in motionless terror, looked as though it had been hung on stakes to be aired. But from a distance they presented a most formidable appearance of six well-grown young men.

The first act of *Pizarro* went off with considerable éclat, but when the Temple of the Sun was presented to the delightful eyes of the audience, the applause was immense.

When this had subsided, the band—one violin behind the scenes, played by Pizarro in full armor—struck up a grand march and the Peruvian army of six men marched on in elegant style and took their proper position to listen to Rolla's celebrated address beginning with, "My brave associates! Partners of my toils, my feelings, and my fame!"

Rolla's address concluded, the band commenced a slow, solemn piece of music. This was the point at which the Virgins entered to begin their worship of the sun. They made their appearance, coming from each side of the stage; they met center stage, then side by side passed up, bowed in salutation to the god of day, took their places on stage and began the beautiful chant of "Oh, Power Supreme."

The first pair of Virgins was the Elvira of the Night, Mrs. Lewis, and Miss Denny, with long white robes and veils to disguise them. The next set was two daughters of Mr. Drake—Miss Julia, then about fourteen years of age, and her sister Martha, about five years older. The third pair was an old Irishwoman who cleaned the dressing rooms, and the property man, a Pennsylvania Dutchman whose business it was to provide all small articles of furniture required for the stage. As the old song goes, "Sure such a pair was never seen." A description of these *virgins* will indicate the many devices and makeshift arrangements the pioneers of Western drama had to resort to in order to make illusion a reality.

Their costumes consisted of long, white cotton gowns reaching to the ankles, and closed in front. Around the waist was a red sash; suspended from the neck by a brass chain was a large golden sun; over the head and ears, and reaching to the shoulders, a white cloth or bandeau; over this a short, white gauze veil reaching below the chin in order, in this case, to conceal the features. The property official was a short man with a low forehead, a pug nose, and in no small degree corpulent. The old housecleaner was not able to make as prominent an appearance, yet when she moved on the stage there was a stern reality exhibited by her that made her as conspicuous in the public eye as her companion.

While this ceremony of entering and doing reverence to the sun was proceeding, it was accompanied by a silence appropriate to any devotional service, Christian or pagan; but when the last mentioned pair entered, bowed, and walked upstage, from the center of the pit came a long, pious groan, and a voice, partially subdued but loud enough to be heard in the prevailing silence, "My God! What virgins!"

The effect was not unlike that of dropping a lighted match into a canister of gunpowder. The explosion was tremendous. The pit shouted and the house roared with spontaneous laughter to which even the actors submitted. It was five minutes before it subsided.

The play did go on, that is, until the tearful Bridge scene of the escape of Rolla with his infant son. In it, Rolla rushes across the bridge, sword in one hand, and infant, held high, in the other. He cuts down the fiber suspension bridge after crossing. His pursuers can not follow, and the applause is tumultuous.

The Drakes could find no one in town who would risk their infant, so a dwarf was recruited to fill the bill.

The scene came: Sam Drake defied his captors and rushed to the bridge with the *child* held high as the stage directions demanded, when a strong masculine voice from above added an unexpected line: "Don't you drop me, you so-and-so!"

There followed a second interruption by the audience.

Old Drake used the extra money made in Pittsburgh to buy complete fittings for the boat. It was nothing more than a floating houseboat. There were sleeping quarters aboard for Drake and the ladies. The men had to find night shelter for themselves in farmhouses near whatever landing had been reached in the afternoon. Although the queer craft was capable of making its way down the Ohio at the rate of some twenty miles a day, because houses were few and far between, stops were made whenever one was sighted, and the trip was slow.

At one landing the boys thought they had engaged an outbuilding of a farmhouse for the night's lodging. While they were dining together on the boat, another flatboat, larger than theirs and carrying mules intended for Southern markets, came down the river and landed a little above their own. Other than merely remarking upon its arrival, the troupe gave it no further thought.

After supper, the actors made for the house. But in the room where they were to lodge sat two mud-spattered Dutchmen smoking their pipes. The room smelt like a horse stable.

It was no use pleading with the farm owner. He had already promised these mule handlers a bed in the same room with them. The actors remonstrated, but in vain. It was the custom to accommodate all comers, the farmer said, and no one should object to the sharing of convenience wherever found in this roughly settled country.

The actors returned to their boat and held a council of war. They were determined to get those fellows out. But how? That was the question.

Sam Drake proposed they should get up the ghost scene from *Hamlet*. If that wouldn't move them, nothing would. Sam would impersonate Hamlet, a character he knew thoroughly, Alec Drake would do Bernardo, and Williams would play Horatio. Mr. Hull would be the Ghost of Hamlet's father, without the speeches.

It was a problem, however, to make the Ghost appear truly frightful. The real armor, such as the Ghost usually wore, would not do. At last Alec thought of the white canvas outfit worn by the animated statue of Don Guzman in the pantomime of *Don Juan*, a piece often played in those days. It was cut like some little boy's clothes with the legs and body in one piece; but in this case the feet were also added, making one undivided garment from the toes to the neck. It opened in the back, through which a person got into it. There was a headpiece of the same material sewed to the costume, which covered the hair and neck. Over this was thrown a kind of herald's cloak of the same material, the whole being left white except for some black shadings which gave the appearance of rivets. The purpose, in the pantomime, was to represent a white marble figure of a man in armor.

The effect was awesome, and slightly ridiculous in this instance, for Hull's face was whitened with chalk and flour and marked with burnt cork in order to look cadaverous and corpselike. James Drake was to bring him to the back door of the house, and at the signal, the *ghost* was to crow like a chanticleer and quickly get out of sight.

Sam, Alec and Williams went up to the house. Sam and Alec sat down in the room, occasionally dropping a remark about ghosts, goblins and spectres, the plan being to keep these men awake. Williams paced outside, waiting for his cue.

The two Dutchmen had taken numerous swigs at a bottle they had brought from their boat and were beginning to yawn and nod drowsily. Their bed being ready, one pulled off his pantaloons, lay down and fell asleep.

At that moment Williams saw the apparition gliding stealthily along through the woods towards the back of the house. Williams, placing himself near the front door, waited for the signal from James. Presently the *cock* crowed and he stepped into the room.

The man who had not yet lain down was sitting on his bed. He had pulled off one boot and was about to pull off the other when, addressing his two friends, Williams began in a very serious manner:

WILLIAMS: Well, has the thing appeared again tonight?
A. DRAKE: I have seen nothing—

SR. DRAKE: Horatio says it is but phantasy,
And will not let belief take hold of him
Touching this dreadful sight, twice seen
of us;
Therefore I have entreated him along
With us to watch the minutes of this night;
That, if again the apparition come,
He may approve our eyes, and speak to it.
WILLIAMS: Tush! Tush! 'Twill not appear.
A. DRAKE: Sit down awhile;
And let us once again assail your ears,
That are so fortified against our story,
What we two nights have seen.
WILLIAMS: Well, sit we down (taking a seat),
And let us hear Bernardo speak of this.
A. DRAKE: Last night of all,
When yon same star, that's westward from
the pole. . . .
SR. DRAKE: Peace—break thee off—Look where it
comes again.

The Ghost entered the room by the back door.

The Dutchman drew back on the bed, the hair bristling on his arm, his eyes opened wide.

"My God!" he exclaimed, "what is this?"

Sam and his companions blocked the front entrance.

The Dutchman, with his eyes on the Ghost, tried to rouse his friend, who only grunted and groaned in response.

"Hans! Hans! Oh, God in Heaven! Hans, wake up!"

He sat upon the side of the bed trembling like an aspen, while the sweat rolled down his forehead in great drops. Sam Drake was delivering the following words, apparently overcome with awe in true Shakespearean style:

145

Angels and ministers of grace defend us!
Be thou a spirit of health or goblin damned?
Bring with thee airs from heaven or blasts from hell?
Be thy intents wicked or charitable?
Thou comest in such a questionable shape
That I will speak to thee,
Say—Why is this? Wherefore? What
Should we do?

The Ghost slowly motioned for them to follow him and began to move solemnly backward toward the door. The conspirators did his bidding, leaving the front entrance clear.

About the same time Hans finally awoke. He took one look, gathered up his clothes and, without stopping to put them on, bolted out the front door with his companion. They ran toward their boat as though the ghost, or something worse, was at their heels.

As soon as they were out of sight the actors threw out the few things they had left behind, fastened the doors and, after enjoying a good laugh, went to bed.

Upon reaching Limestone, now Maysville, they sold their boat, as originally planned, bought horses and wagons and drove on to Lexington. There Drake met his old friend Usher.

They built a theater on sloping ground, and provided the audience full view of the actors. It had a fine stage from which even a whisper could be heard. Comedies were favored, but the classic tragedies were given a competent hearing. Here it was that young Ed Forrest played his first leading professional Shakespearean role, that of Iago in *Othello*.

The location of the theater was at what is now a corner

of Spring and Water streets. From this site, running a mile down to the Phoenix Inn, was a beautiful tree-lined road laid out after the fashion of an English park. It was a favorite spot on weekdays for the sparks to drive and show off their blooded horses; on Sundays it was the favorite strolling ground for the elite of the city. Now it is the freight yard of the Louisville and Nashville Railroad, which marks a strange tale of progress.

Sam Drake, sometimes Bryant, of Devonshire had his traveling "Company from Kentucky," and more than one latter-day star could trace some connection with it. One relationship started by Sam Drake having his brother-in-law, Palmer Fisher, in the company. Palmer had formerly been a well-known London actor. He married and had a daughter, who married a Mr. Lane. The Lanes had a daughter who became Mrs. John Drew, the grandmother of the Barrymores.

*Harmony Landing near Louisville*

Chapter *10*

# A Blessed and Unvexed
# Retreat

While Will Chapman's dream of the showboat was
being brought to life, Sam Drake's dream of a circuit of
theaters in the United States came true. From Lexington
this theatrical pioneer went on to the capitol city of
Frankfort and then to the thriving river town of Louisville, building theaters and establishing companies.

Vincennes was a stop on the trip from Louisville to
St. Louis. Drake's company played a farce there entitled,
*Drowning Men Grasp at Straws.* But the farce became

a tragedy. Jimmie Douglas, one of the cast, went down to the river to bathe early the next morning and drowned!

Louisville was then a town of about 8,000. Its theater was a substantial building of brick and had two unusual features—a rigging loft and a balcony. It was the most prosperous of all Sam's ventures and during his last years all he had. It finally burned down and Drake retired to his farm, a picturesque place twelve miles up the Ohio River. In his younger days at the Devonshire Theatre, Sam had seen and loved the serenity of the English countryside. His home on the Ohio matched the Devonshire vistas in beauty. Harmony Farm was in the midst of level blue grass meadows, surrounded by the highest hills in all mid-Kentucky. The way down to the river is still known as Harmony Road.

The site became a landmark. The spacious brick house was the first of its kind in the county. The spring house was of white marble brought all the way from Italy. Roses climbed the face of the house to the second-story roof; and indoors, a stately and vast fireplace was a noble monument to hospitality. No distinguished contemporary would pass through the locale without making a two or three-day call.

The bounteous board to which they were treated was frequently served on English china colored blue, green or plum. And although there was the adage, "If the devil sends cooks to any part of the world, it is to the United States"—and it is recorded that most tables of the period served up grease and monotony, such did not hold true for the Drakes'. Quite the opposite: the well-prepared meal was always tastefully accompanied by a fine Madeira or claret. Later there would be native whiskey or fruit brandy in the main room.

There the conversations followed the respective interests of the guests: the state of the Union, the writings of Washington Irving, Longfellow, Lowell, Whittier and other contemporaries, the paintings of Washington Allston, the some 2,500 portraits by Thomas Sully. And Drake Sr., a spirited raconteur, would regale his friends by telling stories. One of his favorites, dealing with the theater, naturally, is still told by his descendants:

There was once a celebrated Irish tragedian whose most successful role was Richard III but on his visits to England, his manager had made him follow the Shakespearean text, although he knew the actor's preference for Cibber's gory lines. The scene in which Tyrrel comes to tell Richard of his murder of the young princes, was one for which he had great affection.

Here is Colley's bastard version:

RICHARD: Now, Tyrrel, are the brats disposed of?
　　　　　Speak! Am I happy?
TYRREL: If to have done the thing you gave in charge
　　　　　Beget your happiness, be happy then, For it is
　　　　　done.
RICHARD: And did you see them dead?
TYRREL: Dead, my lord.

Then came the favorite speech:

RICHARD: Get a coffin, bore it full of holes—Cram them
　　　　　both in, and throw them in the Thames; Once
　　　　　there, they'll find their way to the bottom.

At last the tragedian found a manager who'd let him have his way. But on the night *Richard III* was to be given, an actor took ill and Tyrrel had to be played by a novice. With the curtain up and people gathered out front, here is how the scene was run:

RICHARD: Now, Tyrrel, are the brats disposed of?
Speak! Am I happy?
TYRREL: If to have done the thing you gave in charge
Beget your happiness, be happy then, For it is done.
RICHARD: And did'st thou see them dead?
TYRREL: *Dead and buried, my lord!*

Here was a *stopper*. It looked as though the scene might not go on. Throughout the house, patrons who were familiar with the melodrama began to snicker. But the tragedian, set back for just a few seconds, proved as good as Cibber in improvising for the Bard. He summoned all the voice he possessed and bellowed:

"Hark thee, Tyrrel, dig 'em up again!" Then he went on with the dearly beloved lines "Get a coffin, bore it full of holes . . ." and so on to the end.

Conversation having run its leisurely course, the guests would disperse to doze on the mohair sofas while someone played the rosewood piano, or wander through the house admiring its sumptuous but tasteful furnishings. Marble-topped tables and French wallpaper were the vogue; one room was done in silver, one in satin and another covered with elaborate pictures. Unbeveled glass mirrors in heavy and highly decorated gilt frames reflected the scene.

While there were these indications of gracious Southern living in the house, there were no Negro slaves on the farm. The Drakes were not entirely alone in their beliefs; the buying and selling of human beings was as distasteful a business to some Southerners as it was to the majority of the Northerners. Besides, having always been a free people themselves, the Drakes could not conceive of any other way of life.

The Drake policy of employing only free, not enslaved, Negroes may not have met with the approval of their immediate neighbors, but it did not drive the great from their door. In the early days of the farm, Davy Crockett visited them twice; no one was ever able to outtalk or outdrink him. Colonel Breckinridge, who afterward ran against Lincoln for president, was another caller, but the most frequent guest was Thomas Fosdick, the poet laureate of Ohio and son of the editor of the *Cincinnati Enquirer*, who was attracted to Julia Drake.

Harmony Farm had a poet of its own. Drake's youngest son, James, was studying law, but most of his time was spent in composing songs which were to become popular in every household and win him the reputation of the American Tom Moore. "Parles Bas," "Tom Breeze," "Beautiful Isle," "Penser a moi," were some of the titles and it is a pity that but one of them has come down to the present day. "Parles Bas" is an admirable lyric, good enough to be pirated by the lyricist of a long-run Broadway musical.

Of Drake's numerous brood, Alexander was the favorite comedian of all the Midwest; James married a Breckinridge; a handsome grandson had been killed in the Battle of Monterrey. His wife Frances Ann was known as the "Siddons of the West." And Drake's daughter Julia was a noted and beautiful actress in her own right.

Julia married the courting Mr. Fosdick of the *Cincin-*

*nati Enquirer,* and at his death remarried, this time to an actor-manager of New York, Mr. Dean. The Deans had a daughter who, when left motherless at the age of two, was sent to visit her Kentucky cousins. Samuel Drake, the youngest child of Alexander and Frances Ann, became the playmate of the new Julia Dean.

But Old Drake, regardless of his love for the profession, had been determined that the theater should not take all of his family in its maw. Besides having James practice law, he had Charles educated to do advanced teaching. His grandson and namesake was to be a country gentleman and found a dynasty of Drakes in the Bluegrass.

Covent Garden Will Chapman knew that his old friend, Sam Drake, had retired to a farm north of Louisville. But he didn't know its exact location. Late one evening, as the *Theatre* was drifting down the Ohio, they heard a stentorian voice boom out from the shore, practicing lines from the last act of *The Stranger.*

"That voice could belong to only one person," Will said. "This must be the place."

They drew in to the shore and tied up at a small dock with a neatly lettered sign: HARMONY FARM. It was too late to visit or reconnoiter, so the company retired to bed determined to find out in the morning if there really were Drakes ashore.

Not long after daybreak they heard the sound of a fiddle scraping away, breaking off every now and then to give a friendly stage direction. All of this noise clearly came from the stage on the upper deck.

"It's like this," the boy's voice said. "You *sing* 'turn

about,' but you don't *really* turn about. That's the trick of it. Your body starts as though you were going to make a clear turn, but the turn is all between the knees and the neck. You must keep your face to the front all the time. I watched Mr. Rice and he's the best sluefoot soft-shoe dancer in the business. Now, try it again."

The fiddle scratched anew and a child's voice began to sing:

> Wheel about, turn about,
>     Do jes' so.
> An' eb'ry time I wheels about
>     I jumps Jim Crow.

"That's better," said the boy, "but it's still not quite right. Here, you take the fiddle and let me do the steps."

"I can do it better with the banjo," said the girl.

"Well, here. Take it," said the boy. "It's probably off key. Do you know how to tune it?"

"Of course I do," said the girl. "How could I learn to play it if I couldn't tune it? Now you go ahead. I'm watching."

> Wheel about, turn about,
>     Away we go.
> Turn about and turn about,
>     An' jump Jim Crow.

Then a man evidently entered the scene, for a bass voice from the deep South joined the rehearsal.

"You children don't get it right because you don't travel on your turns," he admonished. "And don't give *me* the credit for knowing how to do it. I learned it from a little fellow, not six years old, in the alley by the stage door in Frankfort. Now you both play the tune and watch me."

> Wheel about, turn about,
> Do jes' so.
> An' eb'ry time I wheels about
> I jumps Jim Crow.

The long, lanky body seemed to turn like rubber but the grinning face kept to the front. This queer-looking man, C. D. Rice, was soon to capture the applause of two continents and a sizable fortune as well.

By this time Old Will was up on the stage.

"This indeed is the place," he remarked dryly, looking down at the little girl. "What is your name, child?"

"Julia Drake, sir," she replied.

"As I thought," said Will. "Run tell your grandfather that the Chapmans will be on hand for lunch."

Because of the excitement, lunch at Harmony Farm was rather hastily thrown together. The afternoon was spent by the Drakes inspecting the boat and the Chapmans wandering about the farm. Meanwhile, five people were set to work preparing the evening meal. There were twelve people from the boat and another dozen of the farm regulars. As far as their tastes went, both families were thoroughly American by this time. There were no boiled mutton, greens and potatoes; no suet pudding with porter to wash the whole thing down. First came the bourbon whiskey watered to various strengths, followed by a typical American meal.

Breckinridge, a plumed knight if there ever was one, rode up unannounced. He was always welcome—and presented a fine figure of a man as he stood before the fireplace and with the tones and gestures of an orator mused on the beauties of Kentucky.

George D. Prentice, a Yankee from Connecticut who out-Southerned the Southerners in his admiration for the ideals of his adopted state, rode up for dinner. He was the founder, editor, manager and columnist of the *Louisville Journal.* His editorial style might have been clever, but the Drakes were far from being sympathetic with his ideas. A sample of one of his punch lines was: "They call Abraham Lincoln 'Honest Abe' to distinguish him from the rest of his party." He was a firm believer in the institution of slavery and the only man he ever met whom he could not outargue on the subject was Sam Drake.

Despite Sam's basic disagreement with Prentice, it was a grand evening. After a long supper and a short resting period, the entertainment began. Everyone but Prentice and Breckinridge got up before the huge fireplace and performed something both clever and unrehearsed. Mr. Prentice was overwhelmed by the whole thing. He was especially astonished when Rice, with a child on either side, did "The Essence of Old Virginia," topped off with the number called "Jump Jim Crow." When told that these three performers had met for the first time that morning, Prentice looked doubtful indeed.

Will was immediately interested in Rice, who joined the visiting troupe. He was a minor member but there would be times in the years ahead when he would be the whole show. His rhythmic shuffle was the beginning of the minstrel show in the American theater—a kind of entertainment which survived over fifty years, long enough to give Steven Foster his chance at fame. Indeed, he would have died in obscurity had not the minstrel man created a showplace for his songs.

In the day of his association with the Drake Company, Rice was set down as a "Fly Catcher"—an actor who moves around backstage grasping at imaginary flies while a fellow artist downstage tries to be funny. With the "Jump Jim Crow" number, Rice's ambition began to bear fruit and his dress and deportment off stage influenced the great era of "Black Face." His personal dress was flashy and he used gold coins for buttons. The form and fashion of the minstrel soon took shape with high-colored suits in the parade and invention in song and dancing on stage. The male quartet and the soft-shoe dance were forever inscribed in the American scene. At one time there were ten major minstrel companies touring the country. The climax was reached in "Primrose and West's Masterdon Minstrels with Forty Whites and Forty Blacks." Bert Williams, the famous Ziegfeld Follies comedian, was one of the colored end men. He told one joke and years after in the day of his great popularity when asked what was his one shot at a laugh he could not remember.

From Rice came the invention of the barber-shop quartet singing and many forms of American dancing, the essence of old Virginia, the soft shoe, the buck and wing (of which the Charleston is a pale derivative), the waltz clog, the sand dance, the cane and shovel dances. From the minstrel show up through vaudeville came the skills of such great dancers as Bert Swor, George Walker, Johnny Ford, James Barton and Fred Astaire.

The party broke up. The ladies, children and Rice were off to bed. The two venerable actors, the statesman

*Plate 13*

Caroline Chapman

Plate 14

Julia Dean

and the editor were left to their cigars and talk. It was
a familiar subject to them all—the plays and players of
Shakespeare. The amateurs expressed their opinions and
the professionals set them straight.

First, there was the ever-present subject of Hamlet's
sanity. Prentice thought him mad as a March hare. "No,"
said Drake, "no more so than I think I or you are." "Then
why," asked the man of letters, "the hesitation, the
doubts? What was there but timidity and superstition to
keep him from killing the King when he stood with
drawn sword behind the kneeling man?"

Drake spoke as would a teacher to a pupil. "The scene
comes first into the mind of the author. Invention is a
prime asset to a dramatic writer. If one sees a person draw
a pistol and point it at the back of another, there is a
mental shock. If this happens in a Church the shock is
all the more severe. So, at this spot in the play there
comes to the author's mind the picture of one of his
characters kneeling at prayer and behind him another
with drawn sword. It is a picture that fits into his story
and also two of his leading characters.

"Now the great dramatist and poet shows his art. First
he gets this murderous villain to his knees. How? He
does it with a soliloquy equal to the two well-known
masterpieces he gave Hamlet, with a sure-fire sobering
touch at the finish in the reference to a newborn babe.
How is the Prince to be drawn from the scene? With
just another speech of power, with a reference to the
superstition that a man killed at prayer goes straight to
heaven, and with a rhetorical skyrocket at the finish.
Wait until he is caught deep in sin, 'Then trip him that
his heels may kick at heaven. . . .'"

From Hamlet the talk went to Julius Caesar, with the statesman likening the Roman character to men on the stage of the world of the present day. "I know nothing of that," said Chapman, "but the Bard's characters surely live for me—the patrician nobility of Brutus, the superb thinking capacity of Cassius, and what a picture of the real villain of the story, Julius Caesar, the balding, half deaf, sickly, superstitious, conceited, foolishly ambitious little man! With a superior military equipment already at hand, with himself as historian he has conquered proud people and sown seeds that lead to a blazing harvest in the sack of Rome some centuries later. He now stands astride the narrow world like a colossus to be leveled to a bleeding piece of earth in seconds by the daggers of men he thought were friends."

Following this the delicate subject of Othello was brought up by Breckinridge: Moor or Negro. "Black," said Chapman, "black with Burbage, black with Betterton, turned yellow by Kean to avoid the likeness to Hogarth's tiny Pompey. Thence many middle-aged stars have cut the faults of the man to gain sympathy for a great lover, only to wreck the author's play. Othello is a middle-aged soldier, resplendent in uniform and not inexperienced in the ways of a man and a maid. The poet marked the dark spots of his character and it humanized and strengthened his play. This man accepts the hospitality of a friend's house and steals his daughter in the dead of night. He has won the gentle Desdemona by telling her what Iago notes as fantastic tales about his travels to places where he has seen men with heads growing beneath their shoulders. He is not long past an affair with the wife of another friend. He is not much more the

Noble Othello than his bodyguard is the Honest Iago. He is a lusty man living in a lusty period of history. He has two epileptic fits during the running time of the play—one on stage—a weakling already ripe and as putty in the hands of a man of brains such as is Iago.

It was now nearing dawn and the journalist and statesman left for home to open up their bookcases, dust off their volumes and reread Shakespeare.

The old actors enjoyed their joke and laughter when the two guests had departed. Now they were of an age that could sit up until breakfast time while they talked of the days in London and Devonshire—who was gone, who was coming over, who was in, who was out, and finally about their new country. Neither regretted that he had come over. Both had profited on this side of the Atlantic and both could see great things coming in the future.

Two members of the party did not sleep well that night. Master Harry and Little Julia were stirred by something more than the gala entertainment of the evening. Neither could recognize it, at their age, but both had met their fate.

For the next eight years the *Chapman Theatre* never failed to stop off at the Harmony Farm landing for a visit. The farm was a children's paradise. Julia took singing lessons almost from her infant days and was the Ariel of this magic spot. Harry, with his Stradivarius, played the mischievous Puck to perfection. It was perfectly understood and accepted that Harry and Julia would one day be married. Therefore, when the random wooing became an engagement no one was surprised.

Harry had been born in London in 1822. He had had

a short apprenticeship at Covent Garden in child roles, but he became firmly established in his trade on the Chapman showboat. All young actors then were taught not only to act, but to dance, fence and play a musical instrument as well. Each of the Chapmans and the Drakes could play the fiddle, spinet or banjo, but Harry outshone them all. He did more than merely fiddle. He became so proficient with the violin that he was billed as the "Infant Paginini," after the Italian violinist of great fame.

The famous Swedish virtuoso Ole Bull was touring the States at the time and after hearing Harry play, made him a present of one of his many violins. Years later, when his show was going on the road, he stored the violin in a trunk and left it at the old United States Hotel in Boston. During his absence, the trunk was broken into and the violin stolen. Advertising the loss brought no results, and although it had been Harry's boast that the musical instrument was never made that he could not play, he never struck another note on anything from that time until the day he died.

Harry and Julia were to be married in the summer of 1848. At the time Harry was off barnstorming with some of his pals and wrote his beloved that, right at the moment, he could not quit the boys. The Irish in the blood of the granddaughter of Captain Denny came boiling to the surface, and she sent six words to her affianced in one of those new-fangled telegrams: *Quit the boys or quit me.*

Harry knew an ultimatum when he saw one. He came back.

*Drake Theatre, Louisville*

Chapter *11*

# Journey's End

In what served as his dressing room, living room and sleeping quarters on the steamboat, Will Chapman Sr. sat robed as the ghost in Hamlet. Time does strange things. Here he was in Manchester, Ohio, on March thirty-first, thirty-one years after his first performance in this part with John Kemble's Company at Covent Garden Theatre, London. This role, as well as King Duncan in *Macbeth*, were his own in that company, along with the magnificent Mrs. Siddons as Lady Macbeth and his young son as Fleance. Covent Garden Chapman was now ninety.

His two scenes tonight were all he could get through in these difficult times. The King's instigation scene with Laertes was now on and he could catch a line or two. It was one of his favorites. What a tremendous vitality this short scene had; some of the best lines the Bard ever wrote. Thirty-one years ago this play had commanded a King and a full house. Upstairs now sat the town's few schoolteachers and a beggarly array of empty benches. He tried not to think of it. His mind went on to recall the King's prayer scene in the play, the scene with Tubal in *The Merchant of Venice*, the pipe scene in *Hamlet*, the handkerchief scene in *Othello*, and the skull scene soon to come—all small intimate scenes and all perfect.

The boat hadn't done well this season. Docking fees in the larger towns had soared and the larger steamboats coming in or even passing down the river made the theater rock as though every scene was a storm at sea. How could a performance be given with a handicap like that. And the rain! Two straight weeks of it up to this very night.

His mind went back to his Covent Garden days—how clear the scene was! And how that man George Frederick Cooke stood out. He smiled at the thought of that man, a queer person, but a fine actor. On tour with him one time the company reached Liverpool and Cooke had one of his nights. He floundered about the stage and fell into the wings. Cries of "Apology, Apology" rang from the front. This for the moment brought the actor to his senses. He reentered and advanced to the footlights. His voice was loud and clear as he cried, "Apology to you—never! There's not a brick in your infernal town which is not cemented with the blood of a slave." Liverpool was the outlet for the slave trade to the Americas.

Then the old man chuckled at another thought. It was strange how time could make a thing of humiliation seem humorous.

Cooke spent the last days of his career in America where his success was phenomenal. In many cities the throng about the theaters was so dense and pressing that many were forced through the doors without paying.

Dunlap, the historian, was his manager and traveled with him. The biography he wrote is for the most part a repetitious tale of how consistently Mr. Cooke fell off the water wagon. But Chapman remembered that the critics were kind. One sentence in a review stood clear in his mind: "None could appreciate the beauties of our language until he had heard it from the lips of Cooke."

The old man laughed aloud. Hamlet was not one of Cooke's favorite roles, but he was urged by American managers to play it and finally he agreed, with the stipulation that the Ghost be played by the man who had done it so often at Covent Garden. "My success in that part," said Cooke, "depends on the correctness of the Ghost, and Chapman is my man." So Chapman was sent for. He was delighted when informed that the part was to be intrusted to him at Cooke's special insistence, and he was determined to make his performance realize Cooke's expectations. Actors in these standard parts were given only one rehearsal with the star and at this rehearsal he was letter perfect.

When the night came for Chapman to immortalize himself he was naturally on edge. Being even then somewhat advanced in age he wore spectacles. When the time came for his entrance he, spectacles on nose, was giving his part a last run-through. Responding to his cue, he entered, to the horror of the Melancholy Dane and the giggles of the audience—they had never seen a near-sighted ghost.

Well, he had held the family together and now they were actors. They had mastered all the sound techniques of their distinguished predecessors; and they could play any one of a dozen of the great parts without advance notice. More than that, they could all sing, dance, fence and play a musical instrument.

They were now men and women. The romance of the theater on the Ohio was beginning to wear thin. Nothing had been said directly on this subject but he could feel it more and more as the weeks sped past. Sarah had already married young Hamilton, an out-of-the-family member of the troupe. Their ambition was to go back and play in London. The three grown boys read every newspaper they could buy for news of the theater in New York. Caroline and Harry were no longer children. His work was done. His mind was set. Tomorrow he would call them together and tell them what was to be done.

There was no morrow for him. In the morning they found King Claudius seated in the old chair he had brought from England as dead as the old King of Denmark himself. He was buried in the graveyard of the Presbyterian Church in Manchester and his tombstone stood there until very recent years when a flood washed it away.

The boat and all therein was sold to Sol Smith and the entire company took the next steamer to Pittsburgh, the coach and canal boat to Washington and the coach to New York. Everything turned out as Old Will had wished.

Six years later Covent Garden Chapman's old friend Sam Drake was rounding out his life at Harmony Farm. His had been a long life. As a farmer there had been but small profit. There had been no need of it but it was "a blessed and unvexed retirement" as Bill had once said. All the neighbors loved him and all the great ones of the state were his friends. So were all the animals. A goat and a goose followed him about the place like two pet dogs. The goose had taken a lesson from the camel who had stuck its nose in the Arab's tent. It now slept in the corner of Mr. Drake's bedroom. The scene is now laid there. . . .

A young doctor by the name of Ellard, whose direct descendants still follow the profession of Aesculapius in this very county of Gorham, sat at a table near the old actor's bed. Sam Drake was in his eighty-seventh year. Ellard held in his hand a page ad the old man had placed in the New York *Dramatic Mirror*, announcing that he could send his thespian friends the best whiskey ever made—in bottles or by the small keg—at prices actors could afford to pay. Turning the ad over, he wrote a brief biography:

### A Remarkable Family

Mr. Samuel Drake (known in the history of Western Drama as the Pioneer of the western stage) was the progenitor of a most remarkable family. He was born in Barnstable, England—was educated at Oxford, for the

Ministry; but his association with Byron, Colman, Sheridan, and young men of that ilk, changed his thoughts (much against the wishes of his family) to that of the Stage. His aristocratical training, superior education, personal appearance, and the influence of his literary friends, made his rise rapid in the profession of his choice. Although by birth an Aristocrat, he was in heart a true Democrat—and in the very face of the threatening War of 1812, he sailed for the United States; having married in Bath, one of the professional beauties of the day, Miss Alexina Fisher, and it is through this medium that the Drakes, Chapmans, Jeffersons, and Fishers, are related.

The fruits of this marriage brought forth the following issue—Margaret, Samuel, Alexander, Julia, James, Charles, and Georgina. Margaret was a fine actress, but retired from the stage shortly after her marriage with Thomas Duckham, a wealthy merchant of Frankfort, Kentucky— Samuel was a splendid actor (and considered the handsomest man in the profession) and would favorably compare with such men as the Wallacks, Murdocks, and Davenports, who still live in our memory.

Alexander (known as "Alex") was the great genius of the family, and of his day—his facial powers were unlimited—he could make the Auditory, both "weep and smile," in the moment. He was a Master of the Terpsichorean Art, an expert with the foils, and spoke French like a Parisian. This wonderful genius died in Cincinnati in 1830. His wife (the great Tragic Queen of the West), Mrs. A. Drake, was absent at his demise; and he sunk to peaceful rest in the arms of Madame Trollope (Mother of Anthony Trollope) who, in her "Memories of America," speaks of the great Comedian as being one of the most accomplished gentlemen she ever met. The Legislatures of Kentucky and Ohio adjourned upon the announcement of his death. He was beloved by all—and many an eye would fill with tears at the mention of "Poor Alex," as they affectionately called him. He was not 30 when he died.

Julia was most transcendently beautiful, and was an especially fine actress, in the higher walks of Comedy. Her versatility was remarkable. She married Thomas Fosdick (Merchant of Cincinnati), and by him she had two children, William and Mary. (William was called the "Poet Laureate" of the West, and was one of the Literary Editors of the Cinti Enquirer). Her second marriage was with Edmond Dean (an actor) and she bore him two children, Julia and Helen. (Julia Dean Hayne was one of the greatest actresses of her day—she died in this City in 1868.)

James was an Apollo upon earth—a born poet—and was the idol of the Elite society of Louisville, Kentucky; he married the wealthy heiress, Margaret Breckinridge, a member of the celebrated family of that name, well known in Kentucky's history. A half century ago, his beautiful songs were sung in every household. He was very fascinating in his manners, and called the "Tom Moore" of America.

Charles was an eccentric character—a recluse in his habits—and for 25 years, altho' living within 12 miles of it, never darkened the environs of the City of Louisville —with railroad, river, and turnpike, and plenty of means at his control, he never could be persuaded to do so. When requested, he would say, "What are bricks and mortar to me? Nothing! Give me nature, with God's impress, I ask no more." It is supposed the early death of his sister (Georgina) gave this melancholy tint to his character. He was very gentle, but sad—and the Negroes looked upon him with superstitious reverence. And long after his death, they would assert "dat dey seed him, walking along de river bank." This belief saved the Drake Farm from many raids perpetrated on near neighbors. Georgina died at the early age of 16; she was blessed with histrionic and poetic talent. Rodman Drake, author of "Culprit Fay," was a cousin of Samuel Drake Sr. Dr. Dan'l Drake, and Hon. Charles Drake were also.

The family name of Drake was Bryant, they being the

descendants of Dr. Bryant (who was the Queen's physician) who married the daughter of Sir Francis Drake. Their names were changed to Drake by an act of Parliament. William Cullen Bryant is of this family. Col. A. E. Drake, Samuel Drake Jr., and Mrs. Harry Chapman, mother of the "Chapman Sisters" (Blanche and Ella), are grandchildren of the grand old man—and Clara Fisher Meader was his niece.

In the year of 1854, he died, aged 94 years [Ellard was incorrect], on his farm in Oldham County, near Louisville, Kentucky. His death seemed a triumph over the dreaded monster—I have witnessed many die, but his was the most tranquil that I can call to memory. On the morning, previous to the night of his death, he turned his head and looking out at the breaking Morn, which just began to peep through the veil of night, he quoted the whole of the beautiful soliloquy of "Friar Laurence" in the play of *Romeo & Juliet*, commencing with

The grey-eye'd Morn, smiles on the frowning night,
Chequ'ring the eastern clouds with streaks of light,
And flecked darkness like a drunkard reels
From forth day's path and Titan's fiery wheels—
Now, ere the sun advance his burning eye,
The day to cheer and night's dank dew to dry.

You are better sir, I said—"No! No! (he replied) I am a dying man. I shall never see another sunrise. Well! (He sighed) I am prepared." At midnight, for he died at that "witching hour," he placed his hand in mine, and fixing his eyes steadily on me, said in a deep sepulchral tone of voice—"My son (he always called me his son) this is death. The rest is silence." These were his last words—I felt his grasp gradually relax, and he sunk back into a quiet sleep, a sleep that knew no waking, for he looked calm as a slumbering babe. I called his son, Charles, who was sleeping, and he summoned the household servants—And they gazed quietly and affectionately at him

170

for he was a good Master, and amidst the hushed silence of the night, all Nature seeming tranquil, his soul took flight for

> Then came the hour that all of us dread,
> Which numbers the living, with those of the dead
> When this grand old man, heaved his last breath,
> An eventful life closed, in the mystery of death.
>
> ELLARD.

The final resting places of these two old men have disappeared but they are both worthy of the epitaph of the first great English actor: EXIT BURBAGE.

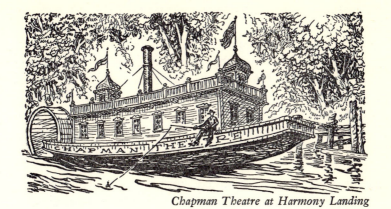

*Chapman Theatre at Harmony Landing*

*Chapter* **12**

# Civil Strife

Mrs. Alexander Drake of Louisville, Kentucky, nee Frances Ann Denny of Albany, New York, had become a name to conjure with. Regarded erroneously as a Western product, she was dubbed "Star of the West," one of the native bright lights of the theater in a rising young nation that still leaned heavily on England for its cultural refinements, its plays and its actors. In fact, the New York critics preferred her portrayal of heavy tragic roles to that of Fanny Kemble, and at one point in her career she planned an invasion of London to carry the comparison into enemy territory.

Fanny Kemble had been the first great British actress to visit the United States and no other actress from abroad ever made such an astounding success. It was just a repetition of what she had done in her native London. *The Hunchback* was written for her and throughout her acting career it remained her favorite role.

With the Kemble furore at its height, Mrs. Drake came into New York and opened as Julia in this Sheridan Knowles' work. The theater was The Park, which had long since seen its best day, and her supporting company was far from being the best that could be recruited.

Here is what the critic of the *New York Mirror* thought of Mrs. Drake:

> She is a fine actress, an ornament to the American stage. She has a noble commanding art and her enunciation is unusually clear and impressive. It brought her into striking contrast with the most extraordinarily gifted female of the age and one whose unrivalled powers has made the character exclusively her own. Yet Mrs. Drake acquitted herself with much ability and many of her points were marked and original.

The contrast mentioned was Fanny Kemble.

She had letters of introduction from good friends like Washington Irving, John Howard Payne, the Duke of West Weimar, and other prominent notables to many of the famous names in Europe. But this most promising invasion of English nineteenth century theaters was never made, probably because Mrs. Alex was the matriarch of several large families which occupied much of her time. And Cincinnati, where she and the elder Drake managed a theater until Sam's death in 1830, became her special domain.

In the mid-1800's the national spirit of progress was strong in every respect. American society had a minimum of stilted formality and the country as a whole was going forward in a most undignified way. At least that was the consensus among certain social leaders thirsting to bring their brand of culture to their countrymen. This was not always a success, and, to one person in particular, Cincinnati was the greatest of failures.

Cincinnati, the *Queen City*, represented wealth, bustling business and refinement. Although some dubbed her "Porkapolis" because the efficient pork-packing industry was centered there, Cincinnati did not neglect the finer things of existence. She published four daily and weekly newspapers and a number of books. A few professional writers and painters resided on her clean unlighted streets. Sixth in national size, she had numerous museums, scientific and religious societies, libraries and medical services. Though of a mixed population, she was the most German of American cities and the German peasant dress of black velvet with red coats was a familiar local sight.

Cincinnati gave generous patronage to her theaters and was fairly tolerant of show folks in general. Her culture may have been a bit raw in spots, but it was there nevertheless. She was willing to have it refined, but resisted any high-handed attempts. Thus it happened that Mrs. Anthony Trollope's attempt to bring *cultural enlightenment* to Cincinnati through the medium of her Bazaar resulted in personal disappointment that left a scar.

The bazaar itself was considered, even then, a prize architectural monstrosity. It was a brick structure with Gothic windows, Grecian pillars and a Turkish dome. And, as if that wasn't enough, the entire building was covered with a rash of Egyptian bas-relief figures.

The bazaar was intended as an outlet for English goods as well as a center of culture. But British goods did not have the appeal and value they acquired later on. In those days, the British mark was more of a drawback than an asset. After the failure of the bazaar, Mrs. Trollope shook the dust of the Queen City from her shoes and returned to England. There she published *The Manners of the Americans*, an exorcism of everything in the West.

The book contained several notes on Mr. and Mrs. Alexander Drake and company:

> The great inducement for theatre-going was the excellent acting of Mr. and Mrs. Alexander Drake, the managers. Nothing could contrast more than their lines of acting, but the great versatility of their powers enabled them often to appear together. Her cast was of the highest walk of tragedy, and his the broadest comedy, but yet I have known them to change character for a whole evening and have wept with him and laughed with her as it was their will and pleasure to ordain. I think in his comedy he was superior to any actor I ever saw except Emery. Let him speak whose words he would, from Shakespeare to Colman, it was impossible to feel the fun not his own. He had, too, in a very high degree the power that Faucett possessed of drawing tears by a sudden touch of natural feeling. His comic songs might have set the gravity of the judges and the bishops together at defiance. Liston is great but Alexander Drake is greater.

Mrs. Drake, formerly Miss Denny, greatly resembles Miss O'Neil; a proof of this is that Mr. Kean, who had heard of the resemblance, arrived in New York late in the evening, saw her for the first time and immediately exclaimed, "That's Miss Denny." Her voice, too, had the same rich and touching tones and is superior in power. Her talent is decidedly first-rate. Rich and genuine feeling, correct judgment and the most perfect good taste distinguish her play in every character. Her last act of Belvidera (in *Venice Preserved*) is superior in tragic effect to anything I have ever seen on the stage, the one great exception to all comparison, Mrs. Siddons, being set aside.

It was painful to see these excellent performers playing to a miserable house, not one-third full, and the audience not including half a dozen persons who would prefer their playing to that of the vilest stroller. In proof of this I saw them, as managers, give place to paltry third-rate actors from London; who would immediately draw crowded houses and be overwhelmed with applause.

We also saw the great American, Mr. Forrest . . . when I saw him play Hamlet; not even Mrs. Drake's sweet Ophelia could keep me beyond the third act.

The theatre was not really a bad one, 'though the very poor receipts rendered it impossible to keep it in high order; but an arrogance greater than the decorations indifferently clean was the style and manner of the audience. Men entered the lower tier of boxes without their coats; and I have seen shirt-sleeves tucked up to the shoulders; the spitting was incessant and the mixed smell of onion and whiskey was enough to make one feel that even the Drakes' acting was dearly bought by the obligations of its accompaniments. The bearing and the attitudes of the men are perfectly indescribable; the heels thrown higher than the heads, the entire rear of the person presented to the audience, the whole length supported by the benches, are among the postures that these exquisite posture-makers exhibit. The noises, too, were perpetual, and of the most unpleasant kind; the applause is expressed by cries and thumping with their feet, instead of clapping, and when a patriotic fit seized them and "Yankee Doodle" was called for, every man seemed to think his reputation depended on the noise he made.

But to get back to Mrs. Drake. None of the bestowed praises were extravagant. America was obviously not the art center of the world, but as far apart as Cincinati and Mrs. Trollope may have been in most respects, they did agree in their opinion of Frances Ann Denny Drake. Her figure and manner were impressive and she had a queenly bearing to match.

There is one other opinion of merit to be cited, that of Joe Cowell, an English comedian. Though Cowell looked upon everything with a jaundiced eye, he was an excellent businessman, which is probably why he lacked the unction for the low comedy parts as they were then written.

Cowell first met Frances Drake in the Green Room of the theater in Cincinnati and had this to say:

> I perched myself on a throne chair by the side of Mrs. Drake, who was seated next to the fire on a bass drum. I found her a most joyous, affable creature, full of conundrums and good nature. She made capital jokes about her peculiar position; martial music—sounds by distance made more sweet—and an excellent rhyme to drum which I am very sorry I have forgotten.

When Lafayette made his farewell tour of the country in 1824, he passed through Lexington, Kentucky. On May 14 and 15 Lexington treated the illustrious Frenchman to the usual elaborate ceremonies given in his honor;

there were fireworks, speeches, parades and, to top off everything, a ball in his honor above the celebrated candy shop of Mr. Bonnet on Short Street. The General and Mrs. Drake led the grand opening march which had its humorous aspects, to one observer at least. He wrote that Lafayette, always a small man, was now, at seventy-four, down to a shrunken five-foot-five and looked like a "plucked wren while Mrs. Drake, six feet and over, was a handsome woman and plenty of her."

Frances Ann Drake had her lighter side even though her private life was somewhat a match for her stage *Tragedy Queen*. Besides, tragedy roles of that time were probably the most difficult to play in the history of the theater and required the greatest of skill. If they were performed today they might seem stilted, but to the audience that witnessed them they were most effective. If the style of acting was broad, the mammoth theaters with their tier after tier of balconies, immense sloping stages and deep aprons were certainly built for it. The one encouraged the other.

True to the traditions of the English theater, the Drakes were ever the givers of benefits. These were specially selected performances in which all proceeds except overhead expenses went to various outside organizations or to individuals directly employed in the theater.

Benefits were given for the water works, gas works, roads, fire companies and for the victims of fire, flood or yellow fever. But once each season the proceeds were for the actors themselves. The artists called upon the patrons at their homes and took orders for tickets for his or her designated night. It was an old English custom

179

sanctified by the most reputable of artists, Mrs. Siddons, who, dressed in a red woolen cloak such as was worn by servants, knocked at each door in an English provincial town to deliver the playbill of her benefit night.

Once Mrs. Drake called upon Mr. Nicholas Longworth, the richest man in Cincinnati, with a request for the purchase of tickets for the relief of a lady recently widowed and left with five children and no legacy. She described the helpless mother as being of excellent character and deserving of help.

"I shan't give a single cent," said Mr. Longworth. "Such persons can always find someone to relieve them. I assist none but the idle, worthless vagabonds that no one else will help."

Frances Ann was surprised but not undaunted. When she left the old man she was in apparent good humor but boiling within. Late in the same season Frances again appeared at the Longworth mansion. She had in tow the most disreputable specimen of humanity ever seen on the streets of the town. He was an aged and tattered tramp and Frances demanded that he be helped, as Nick had promised. Longworth was stunned for a moment but dug into his pockets for a coin. Who wouldn't to get such a sight away from the front of his house? When the identity of the tramp was revealed as being Alexander Drake, made up for his benefit role in *The Ragamuffins of Paris*, Longworth, realizing the joke was indeed on him, bought a box.

Longworth had a favorite place for his afternoon nap. It was under a tree on his great lawn just where the sidewalk turned the corner. Early each clear evening he would bring a chair, place his hat on the grass beside him and doze off. The actors on their way to the theater thought it fun to drop coppers in the hat as they passed by. But Mr. Longworth soon made them cry quits. He collected the pennies and used them to help pay for his theater tickets.

Frances Ann had just become an established success and was away on the road when her husband, Alexander, at the height of his own career, died suddenly at the age of thirty-two. After a long struggle he had at last attained financial independence and was a most beloved public character. At the report of his death, the legislatures of Ohio and Kentucky adjourned for the day, and people cried on the streets of Cincinnati.

It was a severe blow to his loving wife, but to her aid came the control of emotions to substantiate the written claim that she could take loss and hardship with a smile.

Now, more than ever, Frances Ann worked to hold the family together. After the marriage of her daughter Julia to Harry Chapman, and the death of her son Richard in the storming of the heights of Monterrey, and with another serving in the War between the States, Mrs. Drake retired to Harmony Farm. Her acting days were over, the family was scattered, and she was no longer needed.

In the struggle between the States Lincoln had solemnly promised to respect the neutrality of Kentucky and not to interfere with the institution of slavery if the state would refrain from secession. But, as sometimes happens, the sincerest promises are broken by the necessities of a great war. Within a year there were spies and guerrilla forces in every county of the Blue Grass state. Families were torn apart; brother fought against brother. The second year, Negroes were enlisted as Union soldiers and the South protested. A reign of terror began that has no equal in American history. Negro garrisons were stormed mercilessly and there was the fated retaliation.

Hardly a place escaped. The Drake farm was overrun and looted by lawless bands from both sides and no hand could be raised to stop them. Notes and receipts were often left, which were regarded by the theatrical folk as so much stage money.

Neither a Drake nor a Chapman had ever held a slave, but their immediate neighbors had, so there was hard feeling and isolation from the start. Alexander Jr. joined the Union forces at Lincoln's first call. Another son, Sam, volunteered as an aide in the hospitals in Washington. Harry Chapman gathered his little family together and ran the blockade up the river to Pittsburgh, and in 1861 went to New York City. Three nephews from New York State were in the Union forces. Frances Ann had never seen them, but her sisters in Albany frequently sent news of her down East relatives. The friendly Negroes had melted back into the gullies and the hills. Mrs. Drake was completely alone. A letter now in the Harvard University Theatre Collection from N. M. Ludlow to Sol Smith, her old managers, describes her condition as destitute and her situation as desperate. Many in Louisville felt kindly about the great lady of the theater, but there was danger in friendship with those who sided with the Union and few ever came to the farm.

The house stood on a knoll and from the north windows in winter one could see the whole length of the winding road that led to Gorham, a thoroughfare now known as the River Road. In the daytime Frances Ann could watch the approach of unwelcome visitors from a distance of two miles. An old flintlock and a stage cutlass was all she had to defend herself with, but she was made of stern stuff and no harm ever came to her.

One cold February dawn she opened the door of her house to find a ragged man lying on the path that led to the road. His face was distorted convulsively, and his hands were tightly clenched. Without hesitation she half-carried, half-dragged him into the house and propped him up in a chair. From under a loose floor board in one corner she brought a jug of whiskey and, placing it in the man's hands, lifted his arms so that he could drink.

Slowly he came to and stared at his rescuer seated on a chair in the center of the room. His shifting eyes, wanderingly taking in every object, showed that he was fully conscious.

"Who are you and what are you doing here?" Mrs. Drake asked him.

"Madame," he said, in a strained nasal tone; he seemed to have some difficulty in speaking, "I'm a peddler. I started out from Vermont and worked my way down to the southern part of Texas. When the war came on I was robbed like everyone else. For over two years I've been trying to get back home. I've had to hide from both armies. If I could only cross the river I'd breathe easily for the first time in a long, long while. I'll work hard, ma'am, for just a little help."

"There's nothing here that you can do," Frances Ann told him, "and of all the boats we once owned, there's not a skiff left. You might build yourself a raft of driftwood and float your way across. From the weather readings, it's going to be a mild night, so there won't be much

danger on that score. In the meantime you can use the
water and wood in the kitchen. There's a pot of stew on
the stove, all I have in the house today. I give you leave
to shift for yourself. I have my housework to finish."

The man shuffled out of the room and down the hall.
Mrs. Drake replaced the jug of whiskey and started to
dust the furniture and woodwork. She could hear him
put fresh wood in the stove.

In about a half hour she heard him coming back into
the room where she was. He still seemed weak but before
he could say thanks for her hospitality he suddenly became tense. Both hands went down into his rags. He
withdrew one hand, raised it to his mouth and swallowed
what seemed to be a small piece of paper. The other hand
remained hidden, but Frances Ann could see his arm was
trembling.

She followed his glance to the north window. Through
the glass she could see two Union officers galloping
toward the house.

"Those men mustn't find me here," said the stranger.
"I'll tell you why when they've gone. Where can I hide?"

Mrs. Drake pointed to the stairs. "Up the ladder on the
floor above to the garret," she said.

The two officers dismounted at the gate. As they came
up the path she recognized John Silsby and Lieutenant
Griswold, two young men native to Louisville. She
opened the door to them. Their greeting was one of
friendly chivalry. They had seen her on the stage many
times and had met her at several social gatherings. They
had known Alexander Drake and the loyalty of the
family to their cause. She invited them to stay, but Silsby
declined.

"No, ma'am," he said, "we're in a powerful hurry. We've got to cover the main road to Gorham as fast as we can. Perhaps the news hasn't reached you yet, but Colonel Morgan and seven of his men broke jail in Columbus day before yesterday and five of them are still at large. We caught Ralph Shelton and Sam Taylor sneaking into Louisville and I'm afraid some others may be headed this way. You know some of Morgan's men. They've raided this part several times. Have you seen any strangers around?"

"No, gentlemen, I have not. There's been no one at this place for three days."

"There's someone else we'd like to have news of," said Lieutenant Griswold. "A peddler. That's what he says he is, but actually he's a spy; the contact between the guerrillas and the main Confederate Command. He was responsible for the ambush at Mulbach. Fifty men and two hundred horses lost. If we ever set eyes on him we'll hang him from the nearest tree."

The two officers then left the house and crossed the path to their horses. They mounted, waved to Mrs. Drake and rode off.

When they were out of sight, Frances Ann stood at the foot of the staircase and called as from center stage to the wings: "Come down here, you!"

The man came slowly down the ladder, then the stairs and stood before her. Now he was openly armed with a small derringer, as alert and wide-eyed as any hunted creature.

"I heard," he said, "and I'm grateful."

"You need not be," she answered. "I want no fighting or hanging on my place. You may or may not be the spy they say you are, but you're no peddler. You're made up for a part, but your dialect is very bad. You're a cockney. You were acting out on the path there. You weren't spent or exhausted. I had only to start the whiskey to your mouth. Nor were you too weak or hungry to stop and examine those framed programs on the hall wall as you went to the kitchen. You took an even longer look on your way back. Now put up that revolver and tell me who you are and what you're doing on my place."

The man spoke quietly. His voice had a true London ring very familiar to Frances Ann.

"My name is Chapman; Bernard Chapman. Those names on the programs are of my family. I knew they were in America but I haven't been in touch with them for many years."

"Were you looking for them? Were you guided here?"

"No. I am . . . what those men said I am. A Confederate spy. I came—" One look at the change of expression on Frances Ann's face silenced him.

"*You murderer!*" she said. "You killed fifty men at Mulbach; God knows how many more somewhere else. I have two sons and three nephews fighting for their country, and you, an Englishman, bring death to my people! How could you fall so low?"

"I thought of it as an adventure. I was to help Charlie Wyndam. He's a surgeon. I tried, but I couldn't stand it any longer—holding screaming men down on railroad platforms while their limbs were amputated. What could I do?"

"You could have made your way back before you led men to their death! Now quit this place and keep moving. Cross the river as best you can. I'll go to Louisville tonight and report that you've been here. Go now! You take my curse and the curse of your family with you."

Throwing open the door, she pushed him headlong onto the path and slammed the door. She watched from the window. He did not go toward the river. He slipped from bush to tree up the lane toward River Road. When she could no longer see him she went back to her dusting.

Frances Ann Denny Drake lived on until February 11, 1874. She was in her seventy-eighth year and had been rehearsing a small group of amateurs in Louisville the morning of the day she died.

There was no word of Bernard Chapman for many years. Nothing, in fact, until his will was read in Austin, Texas, where he died in 1915. He had kept track of all his estranged relatives. He left a small estate, every penny of which was divided among his various Chapman kin now spread from San Francisco, California, to London, England. His grandniece, Blanche Chapman Ford, became heiress to one hundred and five dollars and sixty-five cents.

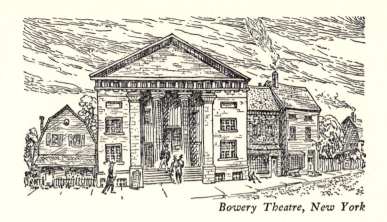

*Bowery Theatre, New York*

*Chapter 13*

# Star-Crossed Lovers

Constantly surrounded by the talk and activity of a theatrical family around him, Sam Drake also wished to become an actor. Although he worked hard, he never quite made it; the gift just was not his. Aided by the family, he played unimportant roles in the Midwest, and once even reached New York in a minor capacity. But an inborn reticence in company and a fear of closed, crowded places held him back and only the farm offered real comfort and peace for him.

Sam had known the farm in its days of prosperity and in the days when raiding hordes of the Civil War swarmed over it and stripped it clean. He saw it rise from the wreck and again stand serene and admired. . . .

Then one winter's night the house went up in flames and he carried his ailing mother to the house of a neighbor a mile up the road. Everything was a complete loss.

But these events were all in the future. Earlier in his youth there had been many happy moments, the happiest being when his lovely first cousin, Julia, then six years old, came to visit, and once again when she was ten and Sam was eleven.

From the talk of the old folks young Sam sensed that all was not well with Julia's welfare. He overheard dark references that saddened his heart but strengthened his love. Julia had been reared by her Quaker grandparents, but there seemed to be a shadow in the person of her father, Edwin Dean.

Julia Dean was a born actress. Everyone said that. On the second day of her last visit to the farm she planned a performance. Sam was the only available leading man and their audience was the little Negro settlement back by the hill. A well-trodden path between two large sycamores served as a stage on which the two young actors strutted and spoke as their elders had in the wordy costume plays of the day.

Both the audience and performers were pleased with the results. That is, all save Aunt Liz, the old martinet of the house servants. She had advanced views on "der drammer" and was not the kind to forbear expressing them.

"You chillen," she said, "is nice to see with yo' love-makin' and fightin'. But the great show in this world is what happens to some people without any of their doin'.

# SAN FRANCISCO THEATRE.

WASHINGTON STREET, BETWEEN MONTGOMERY AND KEARNY.

## MISS CAROLINE CHAPMAN

### IN COMEDY AND FARCE!

First Night of the Infant Prodigies,

### MISS SUSAN AND MASTER WILLIAM ROBINSON.

Second time of Dr. Goldsmith's Comedy of

## SHE STOOPS TO CONQUER!

Second time of the highly successful Farce of

### OBJECT OF INTEREST!

## Monday Evening, March 14th,

The performance will commence with the Comedy in 5 Acts, of

# SHE STOOPS TO CONQUER.

| | |
|---|---|
| Tony Lumpkins, | MR. W. CHAPMAN |
| Sir Chas. Marlow, | MR. MILNE |
| Young Marlow, | ED. BOOTH |
| Hardcastle, | HAMILTON |
| Hastings, | J. B. BOOTH |
| Diggory, | DUMFRIES |
| Landlord, | JONES |
| Slang, | EVANS |
| Miss Hardcastle, | MISS C. CHAPMAN |
| Mrs. Hardcastle, | MRS. HAMILTON |
| Miss Neville, | MISS MONTAGUE |

After which,

### THE POLKA

BY

### MISS SUSAN AND MASTER WM. ROBINSON.

The whole to conclude with the laughable after piece, entitled

## AN OBJECT OF INTEREST!

| | |
|---|---|
| Mr. Simerton, | MR. COLLINS |
| Major, | JONES |
| Primrose, | MILNE |
| Barney, | DUMFRIES |
| Mrs. Vernon, | MRS. EVANS |
| Mrs. Major, | MISS MONTAGUE |
| Fanny Gibbs, | MISS CAROLINE CHAPMAN |

IN REHEARSAL,

### "GREEN BUSHES,"

AND

'FAIR ONE WITH GOLDEN LOCKS.'

Nights of Dramatic performance,

SUNDAY, MONDAY, WEDNESDAY and FRIDAY.

### PRICES OF ADMISSION.

Boxes, . . . $2 00 | Parquette, . . . $1 00

Doors open at 7 o'clock; Curtain rises at half past 7 o'clock.

*Times and Transcript Press.*

CUTLER'S PORT HISTORICAL MUSEUM

Plate 15

Program starring Caroline Chapman

Plate 16

Program starring William B. and Caroline Chapman

# JENNY LIND
## THEATRE.

UNDER THE MANAGEMENT OF MR. H. F. DALY.

STAGE MANAGER, — — MR. W. B. CHAPMAN.

## GREAT SUCCESS
### OF
## DOMBEY & SON.

### WILL BE PLAYED TO-NIGHT, SATURDAY.

☞ IN CONSEQUENCE OF THE

## CLOSE OF THE THEATRE!

It will be played To-Night

## FOR THE LAST TIME,

## MISS C. CHAPMAN
IN HER FAVORITE PART OF SUSAN NIPPER.

## MR. W. B. CHAPMAN
AS MR. TOOTS.

## On Saturday Evening, July 24th,

The performance will commence with the Drama of

## DOMBEY & SON.

MR. TOOTS..........................MR. W. B. CHAPMAN.
MR. DOMBEY..................................MR. EVRARD.
CARKER,..........................................H. F. DALY.
SOL GILLS,..............................................SMITH.
WALTER GAY,......................................HARRISON.
ROB, THE GRINDER,.................................JONES.
CAPT. CUTTLE,..................................HAMILTON.
THE TWO J. B.'S...................................TUTHILL.
SUSAN NIPPER,......................MISS C. CHAPMAN.
EDITH,..........................................MRS. EVRARD.
MRS. SKEWTON...........................MRS. HAMILTON.
FLORENCE.................................MISS EDWIN.

Previous to which,

## A FAVORITE FARCE.

### PRICES.
DRESS CIRCLE,.......................$2. | PIT,.......................$1
PARQUETTE,..........................$2. | SECOND TIER,..........$1.
GALLERY.......................50 cents.

Alta California Steam Presses, Portsmouth Square, San Francisco.

*Plate 17*

Program starring Caroline Chapman

---

# Broadway Theatre
### Corner of Broadway and Broome Street.

BUSINESS MANAGER.........................W. A. MOORE

### ADMISSION ...............50 CENTS

## THIS (MONDAY) EVENING JULY 8, 1867,
### ENGAGEMENT, LIMITED TO 12 EVENINGS AND 2 MATINEE PERFORMANCES,

Of the Gifted Young Artiste,

## JULIA DEAN

Her first appearance in New York in 12 YEARS.

**THIS EVENING**, she will appear as
## JULIA,

A character in which she stands unrivalled, in the late revered James Sheridan Knowles' celebrated Play, in Five Acts, entitled the

## HUNCHBACK!

JULIA....................JULIA DEAN
Master Walter, the Hunchback...Mr. W. E. Sheridan
Sir Thomas Clifford.............Mr. Mackee Rankin
Modus ............................Mr. G. Stoddart
Lord Tinsel ..........................Mr. J. Moore
Master Wilford..................Mr. C. H. Rockwell
Master Heartwell.................Mr W. Goodman
Fathom.............................Mr. J. H. Jack
Gaylove .............................Mr. Jordan
Stephen ............................Mr. Quinlan
Simpson................................Mr. Peck
Holdwell...........................Mr. Berkman
Helen...... .....  .......Miss Hattie Thorne
Mabel, a Waitress  ...  ...... Miss S. Germain
Bridesmaids, Guests, &c.

The Orchestra, under the conductorship of Mr. W. Withers, Jr., will perform, during the Evening, the following Selections of Popular Music :

Overture, "Le Serment,"..........................Auber
De Provizialien Walzer ..............................Bilsse
Cuckoo Polka .......................................Herzog
Pot Pourri, "Nabucco,"................................Verdi
Irish Medley Overture................................Withers

## ON TUESDAY EVENING, JULY 9, 1867,
## FAZIO!
BIANCA ................ JULIA DEAN

On Wednesday Evening, July 10,
## THE WOMAN IN WHITE.

SATURDAY NEXT, AT 1½,
## FIRST JULIA DEAN MATINEE.

### PRICES.
ADMISSION.......................................50 CENTS
Reserved Seats in Dress Circle and Parquette............$1 00
Orchestra and Balcony Chairs.............................1.50
Private Boxes ..........................From $5.00 to $10.00

Doors open at 7.     Begins at a quarter before 8.

Box Office open from 8 to 6 o'Clock, when places may be secured six days in advance.

☞ THE GENTLEMAN'S SALOON, Basement, entrance from the LOBBY, indicated by sign over the door, has been newly furnished and will be found supplied with REFRESHMENTS.—Eatable and Drinkable, supervised by AN EXPERIENCED PURVEYOR

Metropolitan Job Print, corner of Fulton and Nassau Streets.

*Plate 18*

Program starring Julia Dean

Old Life—he the bad man. Him is what you calls the villen. He just sneaks aroun' an' waits until he can beat yo' to the groun'. Look at me! My man whipped me the secon' year we was married for somethin' I didn't do. He ran away an' lef' me with my young child. I didn't do nothin' wrong, but I ain't never seen him again. That's what Old Life done to me."

The flame of complaint died down and Aunt Liz sighed in resignation.

"But I'm safe now. I'm old. That's the best part of the play. When you're old there ain't much pleasure lef', but you can't feel much either, so you don't get hurt."

The children listened respectfully, for both her age and her wisdom were recognized as something they must give ear to. But how fortunate it is that youth will not accept the tragic point of view! The children continued to live in their dream world and with the stamina to make those dreams come true.

At the age of eleven Julia's father took her from his parents to drudge in a boarding house kept by him and his second wife. Julia acted small roles in the various theaters he was connected with in a managerial capacity and in 1844, she apprenticed in Mobile for a season.

The next word the Drakes had of Julia was from a distant cousin, young Joe Jefferson. Julia, he informed them, had run away from home and joined the Placide Company in Carolina. She had stepped in, at a mere fourteen years of age, and played the exacting role of Julia in *The Hunchback*. Swept along merrily on the strength of her instantaneous success, she carried this same role to the Bowery Theatre in New York, where she first appeared on May 8, 1846. The critics hailed her as *the Julia of Julias*. This, in the opus that had been written originally for the lustrous Fanny Kemble.

Sam had followed her, via the columns of the weekly *Dramatic Mirror* which came to the farm, through all the tours of the Deep South. "A beautiful girl," the notices read, "fair hair, blue eyes and bound to succeed and be loved by everyone."

From the companies that played Louisville and went on, he had news of her. It was all good. She was the lady of the theater of her time. Gracious, shy, modest, she was in marked contrast to much of the environment around her. In the far West there was no success as great as hers. In San Francisco she played sixty nights, filling the enormous theaters. In Salt Lake her picture hung in the theater until it was demolished in 1911. An enormous sleigh with her name and with six white horses appeared on the streets for many years after a long engagement there. It was all a repetition of what had happened in New York a few years before. T. Alliston Brown in his history delights to tell that "she returned to New York with twenty thousand dollars as companions." All this Sam heard and cherished. And in the *New York Daily Herald*, which an old friend had sent him:

> A perfect child of nature. We see none of the starched frippery which has been acquired in the Greenroom or by rote in her style of acting. We argue that she will be an ornament to the stage.

Joseph Jefferson, writing years after in his autobiography, delighted in a lovely picture of her:

Quiet, shy, modest Julia—tall and willowy—graceful as a swan . . . whose voice was sweet with the most tender music in it . . . so low, so sweet and yet so audible. It sinks deep into the hearts of all who listen. They are spellbound by her beauty, and as she gives the lines with warm and honest power a murmur of delight runs through the house.

In his autobiography he tells how they were two supernumeraries in Mobile at six dollars a week; how she stepped into a leading part with success on a half-hour notice; how seven years later when he and John Ellsler were co-managers of a stock theater in Charleston, South Carolina, she was engaged and thus saved them from ruin.

The town went fairly wild with enthusiasm. The star was feted and entertained by those to whom she would vouchsafe her presence. All vied in paying homage to her beauty and her virtue. She received these attentions with simple dignity and grace, unspoiled by flattery or success, and in those days of her artistic splendor she delighted to laugh and chat over the olden time when we marched together in the preparatory ranks. The success of this engagement was an event in the annals of Charleston Theatricals.

At the end of the first week we shared $900.00—think of it—$900.00.

Joseph Jefferson was a shining ornament to the history of the American Theater, and wrote one of the most charming of autobiographies. He and his family were very close to the Chapmans and the Drakes. Sam Chapman married his Aunt Elizabeth. Blanche Chapman and her mother Julia had both played in his company and were often visitors at his house in New Jersey. When he retired to his home in Louisiana he kept in touch with them. Just before his death he sent Blanche a painting of his. In many moves worse than Ben Franklin's fire this picture was lost but in the memory of the Ford family it was the same that appears in his book.

In 1854, when Joseph was stage manager of the John T. Ford Stock Company in Richmond, Virginia, he was thought to be tubercular and a very sick man. It was then a stage manager's duty to handle the payroll, and members of the company reported that they were often paid by Jefferson from a sickbed.

He died at the ripe age of seventy-five, full of honors from his profession, with troops of friends and a loving family of three boys and a girl, with a wonderful book to live on for him—a gentleman of the theater.

N. M. Ludlow, who had been in the old Drake Company, was now a power in the South and West. It was he who sponsored Julia, and a great career was in sight; and while no one could foretell with certainty that it was going to turn out that way, her introduction to the exacting demands of a New York audience was the cue for Sam.

This opening must be seen with his own eyes! No printed account, even though glowing, would suffice. Besides, he had cherished the thought of this girl for so many years that he was compelled to go. It had been nine years since he last saw her. He could not have spoken his heart then, even though he'd known it would never change, but perhaps now! But first clothes must be bought and plans made for travel by coach and railroad to New York. Time was short and it would take him all of six days to get there.

Trains in those days were not much better than stage-coaches. The railroad was still thought of mainly as the connecting link between navigable bodies of water. There was small comfort to be found in the rumbling, swaying and jolting over the rough, erratic roadbed in springless coaches at twenty-two miles an hour top speed. Night light was provided by a single oil lamp in each car. Wood powered the trains, causing much smoke and constant danger of flying sparks. It was an exacting and tiring schedule, and Sam arrived on May 8, 1846, the day of the opening, with just enough time to find himself a lodging and purchase a gallery seat before the curtain rose.

Ah . . . how beautiful she had become! And what an actress! There was a clear, round tone to her voice; complete ease in her gestures.

But Sam was not alone in his admiration. The audience, too, hung on her words and applauded every scene. The lines she gave them were particularly suited to the taste of that period. One passage in Bulwer-Lytton's *The Hunchback* was tenderly dear to Sam:

Heigho! I love my cousin!
Would that she loved me. Why did she taunt me
With backwardness in love? What could she mean?
Knows she I love her, and laughs at me
Because I lack the front to woo her? Nay,
I'll woo her then! Her lips shall be in danger,
When next she thrusts them near me! Looked she at me
Today, as never did she look before!
A bold heart, master Samuel! 'Tis a saying,
A faint one never won fair lady yet!
Hang Ovid's art of love! I'll woo my cousin!

Then the last curtain, none the less thrilling than the first. The audience rose and cheered, something Sam had never heard of before. And now to visit the gentle Julia.

He found the dark alley which led to the stage door. But he would not stand *there;* he had heard of the *stage-door Johnnies.* He would stand at the street entrance of the alley where there was more light and she would be able to see and recognize him more easily.

One by one the departing actors passed him by. He could place them in the parts they portrayed in the play. One or two he knew by reputation and any other time he would have spoken but not now. There was but one thought on his mind.

At last the stage door opened again and she came out under the faint flickering light. For one moment Sam's eyes were blinded to all else. And then the beautiful possibilities receded into an ethereal vision.

Julia was not alone.

There was someone with her—a dark, handsome man in evening dress and an Inverness cloak. As they walked toward the street Sam could see how tightly Julia's escort held her arm and how, where the passage was most dark, his lips brushed her soft pink cheeks. She responded with laughter that was like a rippling cascade, as light and gay as in the old days back on the farm, but now touched with the harplike quality of maidenly love.

Sam moved back a step. His form and shadow merged with the darkness by the wall.

She passed within a yard of where he stood, entered a brightly painted, silk-lined carriage with her young man and was driven away.

Sam could not sleep that night. There were too many

emotions, too many self-reproaches to keep him awake. In the morning he bought a newspaper and read the critics' confirmation of her success. She was, overnight, "The Julia of Julias," and there was no greater accolade. He wanted to hope, but could he? How dared he? He let his thoughts run on in a more optimistic vein until, turning to another page of the paper, he read the announcement that Julia Dean was to marry young Hayne, son of the famous Senator from Carolina.

Early that afternoon Sam was on his way back to Kentucky.

The *Dramatic Mirror* continued to come to the farm each week for years, and through it Sam followed the fortunes of the love of his life. Stagewise, a great success was hers from New York to California. She was feted and adored everywhere. The legends concerning her were neither flamboyant nor scandalous. They were frankly poetic. In an age when numerous women attracted attention to themselves by doing the unusual and unpredictable, Julia stood as a symbol of perfection in chastity of character and loveliness of form and action. She personified the current ideal of youth, freshness and delicate coloring as the epitome of womanly beauty.

In Virginia City she opened John Maguire's new theater; in Salt Lake City a great white sleigh with her name painted in red letters was built for her and drawn through the streets by a team of six white horses. And once there was a notice that she had returned to New York from a tour with the incredible sum of twenty thousand dollars!

But all the news was not good. Although a child had been born of her marriage to Hayne, the marriage itself was not a happy contract. Hayne may have admired his lovely and gifted wife, but he looked down upon show people and the requirements of the profession in general. Consequently, he was not the man to share the life she had to lead, and serious differences resulted.

Upon her third return to New York it was revealed the union had been severed by divorce. There were no intimate details circulated as to her private life; but as to her performance on the stage, the reviewers sadly indicated that the original spark had faded.

Sam was sorry for her, but at the same time hope for a future with her was revived. He was confident that his love would restore all that had been lost and he decided to go to New York for her next opening night. Whether or not she succeeded or failed, he would bring her back to the farm.

But from the items he so avidly collected about her, he soon learned that there were many suitors for Julia's hand, and that a Mr. Cooper was preferred above all others. He had been infinitely patient in waiting for the right moment to speak his mind, but Sam still could say, "It may be yet." He was determined to wait until the Cooper infatuation passed before making the trip East.

More news came, but nothing that indicated that she was entirely lost to him—until at last Sam heard that she was to remarry, retire to private life and act no more.

He was at last stirred to action. "This must not happen," he thought. "I can delay no longer." Although his fear of the city was as keen as ever, he would go to New York, go now, to make his belated plea.

He was on his way there when she died.

Sam Drake lived on for thirty years. By then he was old and the sole inhabitant of the farm. He was all but entirely forgotten by the Chapmans and the Drakes, some of whom were in Baltimore, in New York, in New Orleans, in San Francisco and in London.

Many years had passed since his reign as a gentleman farmer of an estate of over two hundred acres. He was a true farmer now, hauling to market twice a week whatever truck he could raise with his own simple efforts on three acres. He had one wagon and one horse, Claudius, a great horse in spite of his age, the last of a noble line of horses.

The family mansion had not been rebuilt from the ashes of the fire which had gutted it. Every brick had been hauled off for use in some other house, along with the blocks of the springhouse, and the ground plowed. The weather-beaten tenant house and a crumbling stable were the only buildings left.

The daily start for market was at two o'clock in the morning, and Claudius took it in his usual stride, one slow step at a time. The few vegetables Sam sold bought food for man and beast and paid the rent of his market space. The taxes could go hang. No other member of the family wanted to take on the burden of the farm, and its sale after his death would take care of the taxes. As for himself, his day was almost done. Old Aunt Liz had said rightly, "When you get old nothing much can hurt you."

The market day was over at six. At that hour he left for Karl's saloon, had a few friendly words with Old Chris behind the bar, and ordered a plate of terrapin stew. The stew cost fifteen cents. A similar amount was spent on three huge steins of beer. And then, to top off these delights, a pure Havana cigar—price, twenty-five cents—the best in the house. It was Sam's one extravagance. He took it to his favorite corner of the saloon, there to sit, to puff slowly and luxuriously, and pass the time. The visits to Karl's were his sole comfort.

Night lowered and deepened over the Ohio. Finally, his cigar burned down to the last inch, Sam stirred in his corner seat and thought of heading home. He waved good-bye to Chris, went out to the hitching rail where Claudius, now impatient, stood, loosened the bridle and climbed into the wagon. He settled upon the hard seat laboriously and clucked to the old fellow to start.

Of late he had begun to feel tired at the least exertion, and before they reached the outskirts of town, Sam, still clutching the reins, was fast asleep. It was more than sleep. It was a wonderful dream. He was suddenly young, courageous and determined. He was afraid neither of crowds nor of acting before them. He was Julia's leading man, playing Sir Walter to her Julia. They were a well-matched team, happy in the plaudits of the critics and basking in the warmth of each other's eyes.

How he loved that speech which so truly described his feelings about her! It was impossible to consider the words part of a play, they were so close to reality.

> A wife, Sir, I can help you to,
> The pearly texture of whose dainty skin
> Alone were worthy baronetcy! Form
> And feature has she, whereon move and glow
> The charms, that in the marble cold and still
> Inspire us! A maid before whose feet
> A Duke—a Duke might lay his coronet,
> To lift her to his state and partner her!

A fresh young heart, one that Cupid hath not
Toyed with, and a warm one,
Mark that, fresh, young and warm,
A mind to boot, wit, sense, taste, Sir.
A garden strictly tended—
Where naught but what is costly flourisheth—
A consort for a King Sir!

Yes, those were the words for her. But even more fitting was Claude Melnotte's speech in Bulwer-Lytton's *The Lady of Lyons*. For in that, bending tenderly above his Julia, Sam would say:

. . . If thou wouldst have me paint
The home to which, could love fulfill its prayers,
This hand would lead thee, listen—a deep vale
Shut out by Alpine hills from the rude world:
Near a clear lake, margined by fruits of gold
And whispering myrtles; glassing softest skys
As cloudless, save with rare and roseate shadows
As I would have thy fate.

It was a full twelve miles to the farm, but old Claudius found his way there, slowly, step by step. He waited patiently at the door of the shack until dawn when Sam woke from his dream.

*Astor Place Riots, New York*

*Chapter 14*

# Merely Players

From the Chapman showboat Harry Chapman moved to the stock company of John T. Ford, the up-and-coming manager. It was there Harry took his young wife after their marriage. He was stage manager and principal light comedian, and Julia Drake, his wife, was the soubrette, their first professional engagement together.

Originally, John Ford had run a small bookstore in Richmond. A Mr. John Kunkle, the owner of a touring minstrel troupe, was playing a date in the Virginia capital when he sensed that there was something radically wrong with his advertising. A parade on the day of the performance did not draw many spectators, but posters were expensive. Still, he needed more promotion. The newspapers that were being hawked on the streets provided a special place in their pages for the "legitimate"; why not try to break in there?

What he needed in that case was a writer to frame his announcements. His search for a literary adviser brought him to the proprietor of a bookstore. He was attracted by the sign John Ford had displayed outside of the shop and was so pleased with the bookseller's talent that he engaged him as advance man.

The next year John became Mr. Kunkle's manager. The following year he secured the lease of the Holliday Street Theatre in Baltimore, and it was not long before the leading stars of the day were playing at his house. When there were no starring attractions available he wrote the plays himself and cast them from his stock company.

The work constituted what was known later as "a grind," and Harry's showboat background and education was invaluable. In addition to running the stage he appeared in the afterpieces and was soon a great favorite in the city. He was known as a prize teller of tall tales. He could top almost any story that came his way, but there was no malice at all in the telling and the professionals loved it.

Harry happened to be shopping among the stalls of the Lexington Street Market the day a riot took place. It was the first week of the Civil War. A regiment of Massachusetts volunteers was passing through the city to Washington. As they came down the street a gang of rowdies set upon them with stones and small arms. Four of the soldiers and several of the hoodlums were killed in the melee.

Harry remained behind a barrel across the street until he could recover from the surprise of the affair. When he reached the theater for rehearsal his story of the riot made him quite a hero. He was occasionally given to exaggerations to bolster his height of five feet five inches. He described the Lexington Market riot as a bloody attack in which only his great valor helped him to fight his way out. As a matter of fact, the only part he played in the quarrel was the part of a man getting hit from behind with a stone while running away.

A great personal sorrow befell Harry and Julia while in Baltimore. Their first-born, Julia, was sent to school at a nunnery in Montreal and died of pneumonia the first winter there. But three more children were born to them to make up for their loss; Blanche, Ella and Prentice. The girls became the "Chapman Sisters," and the boy followed in the youthful inclinations of his father and took up the violin. He was sent to England to continue his studies and later became first violinist with the London String Quartette. He died there in 1898.

In the sixties, with the Civil War becoming increasingly heated, Harry decided it would be wise to move a safer distance from the front. He took the family to New York, where he became stage manager at the old Bowery Theatre.

He arrived in time for the famous Draft Riots; indeed a serious business. Mobs ruled the city for days and many were killed. Even after the more offensive of the rioters were taken in tow, plug-uglies still were against actors on the grounds that the majority of them were of English descent.

At the time Harry was a member of a thespian club whose headquarters were in a house near the East River. One night after a performance the performers were gathered together in their clubhouse, when word came that thugs were on their way to destroy them. Harry took a leading role in showing how the doors and windows were to be made fast. Then he set about arming the defenders of the little fort. To one he gave a hammer, to another an ice pick. He broke a chair and armed four men each with a leg thereof. Then he slipped away with the remark that it was time to call the police. . . .

But in spite of his more than human frailties, Harry never evaded a problem having to do with the theater. There was not a stage device that he could not evolve, and this in an era of massive productions. Stages were often sixty feet deep, measuring almost as much in height. Harry could coordinate a production that had as many as fourteen sets. He was an inventive stage technician, and quite at home in the working of the *star trap*, one of the most difficult stage devices ever created for a comedian—and dangerous. Few would try it.

Two star traps are cut into the stage floor in the form of segmented hexagons. The shorter side of each segment is hinged and fitted with a spring so that each of these parts collapse beneath the stage and then spring into place again. When not in use these parts are pinned from under and can be walked upon with impunity; but when the pins are withdrawn, woe betide the innocent who steps upon it. The comedian was to run, take a huge leap and come down headfirst. If the pins were withdrawn at the proper cue, and if the comedian's timing for the leap was perfect, he disappeared through the stage floor as though the earth had literally swallowed him. The floor sprang back into place, the pins were adjusted from below and the stage was solid once more.

That was half the stunt. The same man who had disappeared into the floor now stood on a spring under the other side of the stage floor and the mechanism was reversed. The pins were withdrawn and he was shot through the air onto the stage; the triangles sprang back into place and were secured from below. When the dive and the shot were performed into one simultaneous action it had a startling and sure-fire comedy effect.

Harry was at his best, however, with Edwin Forrest, an actor of great brilliance and magnitude. Forrest was affectionately dubbed "the Daddy of them all." He played yearly engagements at the Old Bowery, and although he seemed bearlike and rather fierce to almost everyone else, he was most gentle with *Little Harry*. To him, no other actor could sing the music and play the part of the Fool in *King Lear* and the servant in *Richelieu* as could Chapman.

It was for *Damon and Pythias* that these two men of genius evolved an effect that was one of the most sensational sights seen on the stage up to that time.

In the play the tyrant has condemned Damon to death but has granted his last request that he be allowed to leave his dungeon and ride the twenty miles from the city to his estate to say farewell to his dearly beloved daughter. He is to return to the scaffold by sundown, leaving his dear friend Pythias as hostage in his place. The tyrant proclaims that Pythias will be hanged the minute Damon has overstayed his leave.

The scene: Damon's estate. He has bid a piteous farewell to his daughter and now asks the servant to bring forth his horse. But the servant replies: "Master, in my love for you, I killed thy steed."

Damon, after his big speech of the play, drags the servant to the edge of the cliff (upstage center) and pushes him over. The abyss has been pictured in some earlier dialogue as being deeper than the Grand Canyon.

This would not do for the inventive Mr. Chapman. He was, as we know, a small man, never weighing over a hundred and ten pounds. Into his tunic he had two handles sewed, one between the shoulders and one in the small of the back. Made of the same material as the tunic, they could not be seen by the audience. When Forrest, who was a giant of a man, had dragged his servant to the edge of the chasm he picked him up by the hidden handles and, after raising him arm's length above his head, flung him far out into space. The servant fell into a net below, out of sight.

The next scene was just as tricky. Pythias is on the scaffold. The sun has been "rushing down the West" for some time and is now about to touch the horizon. Damon is off stage greasing his face and arms. Just before his cue he sticks his head into a bucket of water and pours the liquid over his begrimed and tattered tunic. He staggers on stage and the crowd cheers the hero and his beads of perspiration. It is probable that this play, once a great success, will never be seen on the stage again, but the movies still use this make-up trick to simulate sweat on the hero.

Forrest was an astute businessman. He made good contracts and kept an eye on every dollar. He left a large estate, the income of which established The Forrest

Home for Retired Actors in Philadelphia, an institution
which survives to this day.

In his youth Forrest held several nontheatrical positions, but a love of the footlights was evident at an early
age. He originated a thespian club and joined several
others. He was still an amateur in his late teens, and as a
minor professional his first real engagement was with
the Drake Company in Kentucky. Forrest learned
quickly. He had been undecided whether to become an
actor or a circus acrobat. Here the die was cast. He was
a hard-working actor from then on, for Drake was an
exacting instructor.

In one of his first rehearsals Forrest had to read:

> Til that Bellona's bridegroom wrapped in proof,
> Confronted him with self comparisons.

Drake, who was directing, asked him, "Boy, who was
Bellona and who was her bridegroom?"

The stripling tragedian was forced to answer, "I do not
know."

"Then," said Drake, "get a classic dictionary and find
out. Never go on spouting words if you don't know
what they mean."

A long time after that, when Drake had become a
venerable white-bearded gentleman, he played Desdemona's father in the same company with Forrest, who
played Othello. It had been twenty years since Drake
was the teacher. During the first rehearsal these lines
were spoken about the magic handkerchief:

> A sybil, that had number'd in the world
> The sun to course two hundred compasses,

In her prophetic fury sew'd the work;
The worms were hallow'd that did breed the silk;
And it was dy'd in mummy, which the skilful
Conserv'd of maidens' hearts.

Othello, pretending to be puzzled, asked old Brabantio whether he could explain these strange words. Old Drake said he could not. Forrest immediately gave, with great rapidity of utterance, an elegant and lucid exposition of the classical superstitions on which the passage is based. He did it with such grace and force that the whole company broke into applause. He then turned to Drake and with a low bow said, "My dear sir, I owe this to you. Do you remember the lesson you taught me years ago about Bellona and her bridegroom? Allow me to thank you."

As he took Old Sam by the hand tears were streaming down the cheeks of both. People in the theater were quite sentimental about their craft in those days.

Harry Chapman was more than a fellow actor and stage manager in the theaters where Forrest played. He was sort of off-the-field spy and lookout for the star. Forrest always kept in touch with the bookings and business of his opposition. He wanted to know what was playing at the other theaters in town and how much their receipts totaled. Harry knew all the doorkeepers. He would drop in somewhere, look things over, and hurry back to Forrest with the news. One swift look around a house was enough to tell him within a hundred dollars how much money was there. On one particular night he was sent over to the Astor Place Opera House to find out what was going on.

There was still a strong anti-British feeling in the country and it flared up in a most fatal way in the jealous conflict between the leading tragedians of the two countries; Edwin Forrest for Brother Jonathan and William Macready for John Bull. Harry Chapman, with many generations of Englishmen directly behind him, was now all for Yankee Doodle.

The two tragedians were in many respects very much alike. Both were men who had worked hard and become wealthy, both had devoted a lifetime of study to their profession and both were egotists with violent tempers.

At first the two shining stars were inclined to be friends, but that ended when Forrest played his first engagement in London and claimed that Macready's business agent and friends had prejudiced the press against him. There appears to have been some truth in this but there is no evidence that Macready had a hand in it. A custom of the time allowed an audience to hiss any piece of business on the stage that didn't suit their notion of what was fitting or proper. It was every American actor's ambition to capture the favor of London, anything short of that brought great disappointment. When young Edwin made his appearance, there were several hisses on the opening night. He publicly blamed William.

About six years after this Forrest played his second London engagement and decided to see the British Isles. He had a box in the Royal Theatre of Edinburgh the night Macready was to play Hamlet. After the second player scene, when Hamlet has successfully snared the conscience of the King and has in jest asked his friend Horatio whether or not he was a deserving playwright, the English tragedian executed a skipping dance across the stage accompanied by a jolly waving of the handkerchief. Whether this was to show an exuberance in his spearing of his uncle or merely to indicate that the Melancholy Dane was a bit unbalanced is impossible to say. It was indeed new. No one else had done it before, none since. How it registered on the audience is not written down either, but it is recorded that from Mr. Forrest's box there came a long, loud hiss. The next day Forrest admitted that he was the man who did the deed and defended his right to do so. Between the two artists from that time on it was "Cry havoc, and let slip the dogs of war."

Just how steadily the flames of conflict were fanned by the press agents, managements, newspapers and professional American patriots is hard to say, but it became quite heated. Display advertising, or *cards*, were inserted in the daily papers denouncing the hated opponent. Both actors made curtain speeches to tell their side of the story. A majority of the intellectuals and society-minded people went over to the Macready side, but the workers were dedicated to Forrest. His strongest supporters were "the boys" who lived in the neighborhood just east of Astor Place. For the most part they were second-generation Irish, as wild as the many generations behind them and with a patriotic fervor to match.

The climax was reached when Messrs. Niblo and Hackett announced that on May seventh Mr. William Macready would play Macbeth at the Astor Place Opera House. The following day Mr. Marshall of the Broadway Theatre announced the engagement of Mr. Forrest in the same play on the same date. Harry Chapman was stage manager at the Broadway.

The newspapers took up the feud and for three days before the openings it was front-page material. On the ninth of May the following letter, signed by forty-eight of the leading citizens of the city, was sent to Mr. Macready. There had been a slight disturbance the Monday preceding.

To W. C. Macready, Esq.:

Dear Sir:

The undersigned, having heard that the outrage at The Astor Place Opera House, on Monday evening, is likely to have the effect of preventing you from continuing your performances, and from concluding your intended farewell engagement on the American stage, take this public method of requesting you to reconsider your decision, and of assuring you that the good sense and respect for order prevailing in this community will sustain you in the subsequent performances—

For the most part the journals of the day were favorable to Mr. Macready. Those who had dared to hiss him the previous Monday night were called *rowdies, ruffians, blackguards, rabble, lower classes* and the *lowest kind of Loco-Focos*, whatever that meant. The *Mirror* invited them to have another trial of strength, and *The Courier* assured Mr. Macready that he was not opposed by any portion of the American people whose approbation and esteem he would at all desire. Ex-mayor Horn, in his famous diary, had his say in a sentence like this: "One is a gentleman, and the other is a vulgar, arrogant loafer with a pack of kindred rowdies at his heels."

The sequel proved that they did not esteem sufficiently the strength of Macready's opponents nor the depth of feeling which had been excited against him. The distinguished signers of the letter and their friends were no match for "the boys."

Mr. Macready consented to play again after the receipt of the letter. Thursday night was fixed for his reappearance in *Macbeth*. Both parties prepared for the struggle. It was to be a trial of strength—"Aristocracy and the English Clique versus the Lower Classes." The signers of the letter called upon Mayor Woodhull to act, and prepared to protect the theater in case of riot. They also bought tickets and distributed them freely for the purpose of securing a favorable reception.

In the meantime their opponents were not idle. Bills couched in language adapted to excite prejudice against the Britisher were posted about the walls of the city. They were very hostile. The following is an example:

WORKING MEN

shall

AMERICANS OR ENGLISH RULE

in this city?

The crew of an English steamer have
threatened all Americans who shall dare
to express their opinion this night at the
English Aristocratic Opera House!!

We advocate no violence, but a free expression
of opinion to all Public Men.

WORKING MEN! FREEMEN!!

stand by

YOUR LAWFUL RIGHTS

American Committee

On the fateful morning of May tenth the advertising in the newspapers and the billing on the streets ran side by side. They read:

ASTOR PLACE OPERA HOUSE

Directors

Messrs. Wm. Niblo & Jas. H. Hackett

This evening will be performed

MACBETH

*Macbeth*, Mr. Macready          *Lady Macbeth*, Mrs. Pope

BROADWAY THEATRE

Proprietor, E. A. Marshall

This evening will be performed

THE GLADIATOR

*Spartacus*, Mr. Forrest          *Julia*, Miss Wallack

The new mayor of the city, Mr. Woodhull, had no inkling of what was to happen that night. There was, however, enough excitement about the matter to cause the detailing of three hundred policemen to the Opera House and the ordering of two regiments of the National Guard to be ready, fully armed, at the armory. The Opera House itself was alerted for trouble. There was a double guard at every door and many windows were barricaded.

The doors were opened and the crowd immediately filled the house. When the doors were closed, the crowd outside claimed that the only ones to get into the theater were those who held tickets with a secret, private mark of the Macready faction. This was not a fact.

The crowd outside tried to batter down the doors. They were stopped by the police, but all the lamps were smashed and all the windows that had been left unbarred were broken.

Inside, the play commenced amid a storm of cheers and hisses. The clamor grew while the play proceeded. At the beginning of the second act, a man dropped from the parquet to the stage. Others prepared to follow when the police, out of uniform and stationed throughout the house, were given a signal and went to work. Quickly they threw out of the theater all disturbers they could find and the doors were closed again promptly.

This maneuver did more harm than good. Those ejected had paid for their seats and their anger was added to the growing fury of the mob outside. In front and rear the mob pounded on the doors and the thunderous noise terrified those inside. The shouts and yells of the mob could be heard for blocks around. The ferocity with which they now assailed the theater drew cries for the police and the military. Such cries were not un-answered.

The Seventh Regiment marched down Broadway, a body of mounted horsemen in the lead. At Astor Place they were greeted by a volley of sticks, stones and bottles. The horses could not be controlled and were withdrawn. The infantry stood its ground. It was doubt-ful if the Seventh Regiment would obey an order to fire on their countrymen. For the most part, they were of Irish extraction, and their sympathies were with the other side. Even their leaders had no stomach for such a brawl and were not inclined to give an order to fire until the last moment. However, the troops, exposed to such incessant and dangerous pressure without the power to defend themselves, could not be held in check forever. The roaring mob was now within forty feet of them.

The officers stepped forward to harangue and plead with the rioters to disperse. The only response was hoots, yells and more volleys of stones. The terrible alternative grew nearer and nearer. The mob was warned again that an order to fire would be given if they did not desist. Only those at the front line of the mob could hear and their replies were, "Fire and be damned!" "Fire if you dare!" "To hell with your guns!" "Shoot away, you sons-of-bitches!"

One grimed rioter with a theatrical flair stepped within a few feet of the ranks, bared his hairy chest and shouted, "Take the life of this freeborn American for a bloody British actor. Do it, you counter-jumping bastards, you chalk-livered, oakum-faced rats. All together now, boys. Have at them!"

By this time the police were in the midst of the mob, singling out separately the noisiest of the rioters and working them to the edge of the crowd where they could be hustled off to jail. This held back further the order to the soldiers to fire. Throughout the crowd fights were going on between the police and the most violent of the rioters and it became necessary to wait until the police could be recalled.

Finally the order was given to fire.

A single musket on the extreme left responded.

"Fire!" was again shouted above the yells.

Three more pieces on the right were discharged; the

shots were fired high in the nature of a warning. Then there was a wait of a half minute. The yells continued and the third order to fire was given. There was no mistake this time. Bodies fell at the edge of the mob, and the rest of it dispersed. Macready, in disguise, had been spirited out through a side door and hidden in the private house of a friend.

That night Harry Chapman rung up the curtain on *The Gladiator* of Mr. Forrest, and figured he could be absent for an hour on his mission of espionage before it became necessary for his return to lead the stage mob at the rise of the third act curtain. To get a complete report he had to run over to the Astor Place and back. The theaters were a full mile apart. He heard the tumult and the shouting from almost the moment he started out. Rounding the corner of Tenth Street, he caught his first sight of the roaring mob as the first single shot was fired. By the time the third volley rang out he was halfway back to the Broadway Theatre. He reported to Forrest that the Astor Place Opera House was in flames, that there were over three hundred dead sprawled about the streets, and that there was about fifteen hundred and fifty dollars in the house.

It was not as bad as all that. Many had been wounded, but the dead in this disgraceful affair counted up to an even thirty. A black page in the history of the theater and the country was written with the Astor Place riots.

J. N. Ireland, in his *Record of the New York Stage*, has this to say of Harry Chapman during his time in New York:

The next evening Mr. E. Eddy made his first appearance in character roles in New York as Othello, and Mrs. H. Isherwood appeared in *The Nabob for an Hour,* thus completing the role of performers, among the best of whom were W. B. Chapman and his nephew Harry. The latter though somewhat of a stranger, possessed great versatility and was soon an acknowledged favorite. He was the son of William, brother of Samuel Chapman, first husband of Elizabeth Jefferson, born in London in 1822, and made his first appearance on the American stage as Coachman Pat in the opera *Cinderella* when first produced at the Walnut Street in 1830. He afterward became a great favorite in Cincinnati, where he was at one time manager. In 1862 he appeared at the old Bowery Theatre, where he was still engaged at the time of his death, May 22, 1865. He had played the preceding evening and was preparing to leave his home for the theater at the time of his demise, when, feeling faint, he threw himself on his bed and in a very short period expired. "For honesty and probity he was second to no man in the profession."

Harry *must* have been important to get this much from grouchy old Ireland.

Julia, Harry's wife, held the family together. Seconded by her mother, she refused to allow her rich relatives in Albany to adopt their two lovely girls. They had been started in the profession and it was her wish that they should remain there.

When the girls became stars as the "Chapman Sisters," Julia herself kept to the faith and became a singing character actress in the operetta field, then approaching its heyday. At the age of seventy-seven Julia toured the country in support of Emma Abbot, leading light opera prima donna of the day.

*Jenny Lind Theatre, San Francisco*

## Chapter *15*

# A Far-Off Shore

William B. Chapman, son of Covent Garden Sam, was a silent partner to his brother Sam in the management of the Walnut Street Theatre in Philadelphia, but he seldom acted there. Instead, he became almost at once a favorite in New York as comedian and singer of comic songs. His delivery won a large following. Frank Chanfrau saw him create a New York fireman in an afterpiece and copied the costume, manner, and make-up to garner himself a tidy fortune in *A Glance at New York*, the greatest success of that decade.

Will and Caroline arrived in San Francisco to find the

dwindling legitimate theater in a seasonal slump. But the mining towns were flourishing and so they took to the road, being teamed with George Chapman on several occasions.

Playing the mining camps was very lucrative for many groups of players. But there were always elements of danger present—the hardships of travel, the possibility of highwayism, and conditions in the camps themselves. These were seething beds of reckless humanity where crime, deep despair, excessive gayety and reckless courage all ran counter. The miners were song-conscious and often put over a number with more ribaldry or tearful sentiment than some of the visiting vocalists. They rewarded handsomely those of the entertainers who pleased them; they tossed those who didn't in blankets.

Edwin Booth was in the Chapman company that toured the mining camps of California. He was a prince in character off stage as well as on, from his early days down to the end. His private pension list of old, worn-out thespians was long and generous.

One bright afternoon, Will and Booth were resting on the porch of the hotel where they were lodging in Sacramento. With chairs tilted back against the wall, they were at ease and engaged in a game of trying to quote lines of Shakespeare which the other could not continue.

A young lass was just about to pick her way across the street without soiling her skirts as Will recited four lines of the Bard's poetry. Edwin was to pick up the cue with:

> Thou art thy Mother's glass
> And she in thee brings back

*Plate 19*  Blanche Chapman

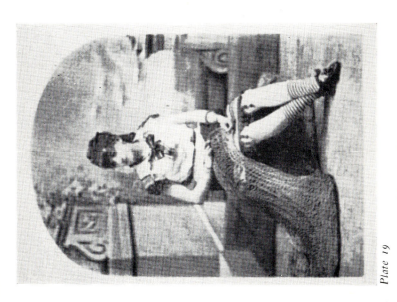

*Plate 20*  Ella Chapman

*Plate 21*

Edwin Booth

*Plate 22*

John Wilkes Booth

The lovely April of her prime
And—

The chair came down to the porch floor with a bang. "Gad!" he said next, and not to quote, "what a pair of gams!" The *Prince of Hamlets* was quite a human being.

Following this tour of the camps the Chapmans returned to the city on the coast. With the exception of one trip to New York, they were to be held by it the rest of their lives, by the splash of waves, the gray mornings, the misty nights, the wind that often blew so fresh and clean.

It is a tradition that every Englishman in a foreign land has a longing to go back to the Old Country; but once at the Golden Gate the Chapmans never felt the pangs of geographical discontent. They had seen both attractive cities and stirring times, but never a scene of color and adventure like this with more than one overtone of old London itself. San Francisco had, and still has, a feeling for the dramatic, a passion for pageantry.

Gold was discovered in California in 1848. In 1849 the rush began. The first few months after the discovery San Francisco seemed to be a deserted city. Everyone had gone to "the diggin's." Soon the whole country was seething with excitement. Ships were being loaded with Argonauts all along the Atlantic coast. In the Middle West people were selling all their worldly goods to make the long, long trip.

There were three routes. The one around the Horn was the safest but it took three long months, while other folk out in the promised land were already digging up

fortunes. The second was to sail to the Isthmus of
Panama, go by wagon or mule-pack twenty-five miles
to the Pacific, and then sail on to the Golden Gate. The
Isthmus was a dangerous hurdle. Mosquitos, fever and
brigands were never absent and many were the poor ad-
venturers who got no further. The third was overland.
There was a scarcity of water, the Rocky and Sierra
mountains to cross, cold and snow, and tales of scalp-
hungry Indians. Few had experience in this sort of thing.
Many useless things were carried only to be thrown
away. There were large purchases of whistles to be blown
when it was necessary to let the other members of the
wagon train know that the Indians were coming.

In the first years of the gold rush the actor and
the miner were not the only ones to make their way to
the Eldorado of the West. All sorts of men and races
came from all quarters of the globe. The roads were
filled with their wagons, the trails with their horses, the
harbor with their craft. From the earliest time the Chinese
came in goodly numbers. Everyone soon found he made
a good cook, a careful laundryman, a sharp gambler and
an honest trader. Men from the southern states and those
fresh from the liberation of Texas flocked in with their
Bowie knives and six-shooters. There were Turks with
their fezzes and Indians with their heads wound with
spotless linen.

More dangerous than all other groups were the Aus-
tralians. Many of those were convicts dumped from
England. They formed a settlement of their own in a
corner of the city and were a constant source of terror
to the populace, which kept advancing in numbers by
leaps and bounds.

Robberies, shootings and stabbings were daily diversions. Groups of idlers hung about the streets at night to gape at the Concord stages with curved bodies and high wheels, and for the excitement of seeing the killings. They had not long to wait before the *rat-tat-tat* of shots would come from some saloon or dive. Crowds would surge to the spot to witness the outcome. What courts there were fell far behind in their work. It grew difficult to enlist police; so many of their number met death on the streets.

It is difficult to get accurate figures on the growth of the population, but it is probable it jumped from twenty thousand to seven or eight times that figure in the ten years following the discovery of gold.

But public improvements did go ahead, albeit slowly, and temples of religion raised their spires against the hills. All drinking places were not saloons with brothels attached, and all eating places did not feature *leg shows* while the footlight candles burned blue through the heavy smoke. There was one restaurant called the "Fountain Head" which, though dedicated to 100 percent temperance and decorum, needed to employ a staff of over a hundred people to keep up with its trade.

Naturally, in a city which attracted so many men there never seemed to be enough women, but what women there were had a sparkle that more than made up for their lack of numbers. Dresses were being shipped from Paris as early as 1853 and ladies dressed in Parisian finery were followed respectfully down the streets. Their groups of admirers were by no means all nineteenth-century wolves. There were no quick changes in the fashions. Ladies' garments were made to last in those days and some of them existed as curiosities to a very late time. Formal evening dress aped the hourglass and the brocades were so sturdy that they actually *stood alone* as the saying goes.

Men decked themselves out, too, with more color than they wear today. There were fancy silk vests, and some even of sealskin, with scarfs and cravats of all colors of the rainbow. Such an array of men's hats has never been seen in any other city of the world. The coonskin hat from Kentucky hung around until it was completely worn out, and transplanted gentlemen from the East wore their stovepipe hats daily. Every day was important and a reason to parade, either singly or en masse. Numerous companies of National Guards, all in dazzling uniforms and the colors of their respective units, were ready to march at the drop of anyone's baton.

The flowering of the theater in San Francisco between 1851 and 1861 has probably never been equaled elsewhere, unless in London some two hundred years earlier. San Francisco, a city of flux and ferment, went slightly mad in its zeal for entertainment. The rough-and-tough and genteel alike wept over sentimental ditties. The gold-rich responded to that which pleased them by hurling nuggets, gold coins and even gold watches on the stage. They were later to pay as high as $500 a seat for the opening night of the energetic and robust Edwin Forrest's Shakespearean season.

Never since Henslowe and Burbage competed in old London Town were theaters built, burned and torn down in such short order. In ten years as many as ten sumptuous homes of the drama and opera were built and almost a thousand major dramatic or opera works offered to the

citizens of the Golden City. Names to be remembered
are the Metropolitan, the Adelphi, the Jenny Lind, the
American, the Old California, the Atheneum, the Ly-
ceum, and the Bella Union whose theatrical output has
never been surpassed for vulgarity. Some of the houses
were of monstrous proportions, hung with rich draperies
and adorned with handsome lamps. Seating capacities
ran as high as the present Metropolitan Opera House in
New York, and the stages had a depth of up to sixty feet.
The city well-earned its eventual reputation of being a
swell show town.

Similarly magnificent were the productions presented
therein. The leading artists furnished their own costumes and, as good artisans and clever competitors, were
careful to have them made as beautiful and authentic as
possible. Every actor and actress had a fine collection of
costumes and stage jewelry, the latter for the most part
bought in France. French paste, it was called, and for the
short life of its popularity did its best to outshine the
real thing.

It was no wonder that the golden city on the Bay
appealed so entrancingly to all those who came in contact
with its spell. And the world of the theater and those who
lived it were no small part of that enchantment, even
though it must be honestly admitted that the acting itself
frequently left much to be desired. This is not surprising
when we learn that few, if any, of the early favorites had
any real training in the art, from the gaming-house entertainers to those who struggled with the finer passages
of grand opera.

There never was such a gathering together of barroom
artists and curbstone promoters, with freaks and fakes

aplenty. Onto this scene came one of those miracle men who often take a sudden hand in the history of the theater. Thomas McGuire had been a cab driver and then a bartender in a saloon in the lobby of a New York theater. He could neither read nor write, but he was a born promoter. Sailing into San Francisco during the gold rush, in no time at all he began to build pretentious playhouses—of which one was the imposing Temple of Thespis—and to engage the most noted actors and actresses from the East to tenant them. He built and named a theater the Jenny Lind, even though the thrush herself never visited San Francisco. It was atop his saloon on Portsmouth Square and was consumed by fire and rebuilt three times in the space of three years. He knew the talent of the Chapmans and they were forever grateful for the opportunity he gave them to become favorites of the town.

All this was well, but as always after a boom there came a nation-wide depression. Its severity was felt more sharply on the West Coast than in any other section of the country. Time and again gas-lit theaters burned to the ground and the active center of the city moved slowly from the streets surrounding the gay park where all the splendid opera houses had been built. Locations changed, and so did fortunes.

Thus it happened that when George Chapman came East for his last New York engagement he was to see for himself how the wheel of chance sometimes makes a full spin around.

He stepped into the lobby of the Old Bowery Theatre one night for a glass of what was then known as *tanglefoot*. He called his order and, except to notice that a gentleman at the right seemed to be of great age, paid no further attention to the man until he laid down a coin on the bar and it was shoved back to him.

"Devil a cent you'll spend here," said a voice the actor could never forget. "It's all on the big house, Portsmouth Square."

Tom Maguire had come back to the same New York theater from which he'd started . . . but he had risen in the world; from behind the bar to in front of it.

Yes, a lot of them came and went, but when William B. Chapman came into his own he went down in history as the lovable Uncle Billy. It was a mutual admiration. As his early escapades have indicated, William had tried hard to keep young; youth was his passion, and the passions of youth diminished but were not forgotten. He passed himself off as fifty-four, for a most particular reason, as we shall see, when in truth he was a good twenty years older.

The Chapmans and the Booths were among the few actors in this period who had a theatrical background, training and natural ability. The Booths—the younger and the elder—appeared on the San Francisco stage with the Chapmans for a time from the end of July, 1852. There were no thespians to equal them until Julia Dean appeared in 1857.

In the great days of its early glory there were several freakish denizens of the stage who need not be appraised for true histrionic talent. There were some vivid and powerfully minded individuals who had their brief hour.

During the years of the Gold Rush the rising population seemed to care nearly as much for the theater as for wealth. One of the first buildings that went up in a mining town was a theater. Much of the entertainment offered was dross that would not have existed for more than a week except in the wild and woolly days of this early excitement.

A glance at the names and qualifications of some of the performers will give an idea of the theatrical fare. Mr. Richard Stark and his wife were quick, but not finished, producers and actors in classic repertoire. While playing every night they could open *King Lear* in eight days, a play in which neither had ever appeared. It took actors like Edwin Forrest and Robert Mantell five years of study before they would attempt the part.

A little girl of six played Hamlet with success and other little girls of ten and eleven played the Melancholy Dane and then put on a mustache and a hump and played Richard III. One child enacted a roaring melodrama called *The Corcian Brothers*, an opus of Boucicault's, and improved Dion's version by doubling the two leading parts. Young ladies played Romeo quite frequently.

Lola Montez, an Irish beauty, had been the mistress of the King of Bavaria and he had created for her the title of Countess of Landsfeld before casting her off. This also created an air of notoriety but it did not give birth to any talent for the theater. She was a failure as a dancer and an actress in London and New York, but San Francisco opened wide its arms in welcome.

What she lacked in histrionic ability, she made up for in her flair in the art of getting talked about. She walked the streets of the city with two greyhounds on a leash and an enormous parrot on her shoulder. She had a strange taste for pets. At her home in Grass Valley she had two bears chained to posts on both sides of her front doorway. They chewed the arm of one of her best husbands and he never darkened her door thereafter.

Catherine Sinclair, an actress for but one season, riding high on the notoriety of a long, drawn out divorce case against Edwin Forrest, played all the leads of most of the standard plays of the day, and was accounted a great actress. She was another born promoter, with a keen business sense. So was Laura Keen, but they both lacked the divine spark on stage.

The beauty and charm of another young Irish lass made her a sparkling favorite, but she lacked the experience for the demanding leads of that time, until years later she returned from France with a dramatization of *Camille* and reigned as a star for many years. Her name was Matilda Heron and she is the grandmother of our Gilbert Miller.

Another adept at advertising was Adah Menken, who won great fame in one of Payne's concoctions. Before appearing on stage in the evening she walked the streets by day in a single garment of fine yellow silk. The big scene in the bad melodrama, *Mazeppa*, was where Adah, attired in a full-length suit of tight-fitting cotton underwear, was strapped on the back of what was supposed to be a wild untamed stallion and driven out to the desert where starvation would end it all. The horse was really a gentle old mare which ambled up a ramp upstage where her trainer waited with lumps of sugar. Nevertheless nothing drew them into the theater in those parlous times like a horse on the stage and a lady in a one-piece suit of cotton underwear.

There was, however, some experienced and skillful

acting of the English classics and some excellent operatic singers and dancers. Old Booth was but a ruin of his former self, but a noble one. Mrs. Judah, almost direct from the loss of her husband and two children by shipwreck, was for years the last word in character women, as was Uncle Billy Chapman of character men. Clara Fisher, a relative of the Drakes, was an extremely clever actress in limited channels. James Murdoch, whom Joe Jefferson, after praising highly in his autobiography, notes that he was "too modest," proved his true worth by going to London and scoring a brilliant success.

The two Booth Boys had learned their craft and were at their height in looks and physical strength.

Lotta Crabtree was the ingénue of all ingénues but nothing more than that. She was an incomparable soubrette who made up in personality whatever she lacked in dramatic accuracy. Beautifully managed and advertised, she became the pet of the continents and amassed a great fortune.

Kate Denin was another Coast favorite of the time. Her success stemmed from a showmanlike projection of stunts, something that suited the taste of this theatrically green and hungry town. But the paragon of actresses, the quintessence of stage talent, was Caroline Chapman.

One actor can sometimes raise the standard of a whole company, and either Uncle Billy Chapman or Caroline seemed to do it every time; appearing together, there was no doubt. They held forth as a team for many successful months, one year into the next. It has been said rightly of them that "No actors ever gave so abundantly of their talents."

Uncle Billy, much farther along in years than was

known, had neither the strength nor the appearance to enact the heroic roles, but in the comedy parts of the genius of Stratford-upon-Avon there was full praise and never a single line of criticism. His salary was high and he saved it, buying himself a beautiful spot of land up in the Napa Valley.

While San Francisco was indeed the pearl of the Pacific, it did not progress alone. In no time at all it seemed that the mining camps had all grown into towns of substance. After the hotel and the saloon, the next thing to be built was always the theater; and as the community grew, so did the temple of the drama. The citizens took pride in having their house of amusement talked about as *a gem*, a replica of some famous theater in Europe, or at least rivaling one back East.

The day had passed when pouches of gold nuggets were thrown upon the stage at the curtain. The days when George Chapman and his family gave a performance on the sawed-off trunk of one of the big trees at a mining camp would never come again. No longer could the moppets of the Chapman clan keep themselves in spending money by sweeping up the gold dust before the store counters where the miners did their trading.

The times, in truth, had changed, but to the Chapmans of the Golden West, the profession was the same as it had been on the showboat and long before the showboat —a trade, a way to make a living. They were paid good salaries because they too, went along with the times, and they wisely put some of their earnings to good use. With the home now built at Napa, they could come down to San Francisco and play whenever they were sent for, in the city or out on the road. They were not too particular about the parts. They were good and could hold their own in almost any assignment.

When they did get into San Francisco, Uncle Billy enjoyed being a noted character in a city of noted characters. It pleased him, when walking down Market Street one day, to hear a father say to his young son, "Always remember that I have pointed out to you on this street William Chapman."

He grew thinner each year and was a far cry from the spark who had suddenly departed old London Town. It worried him a little to realize that his clothes no longer fit. Down at the market one day he stepped on a scale and off again quickly when he found he could not lift the bar with the weights already set at one hundred and ten pounds. It was a further shock when one of the youngsters measured him for height one evening and he had shrunk a good three inches.

Still, Uncle Billy was not an actor who needed inches or pounds. They didn't pay the salary he asked for that.

And so now he lived at his ease, but, as in every actor, his ambition never waned. He always hoped he would create—yes, that was the word, *create*—another leading part, one more title role. He was sure that if he could find the right vehicle he could get Tom Maguire to put on the play for him. Just give him time to study it, with some scenes to play with Caroline, and it would outrun anything yet seen on the Coast!

Finally news came that a certain Mr. Dickens was creating a furore all over the English-speaking world with his novels. People could hardly wait for the chapters to come out each month. William read them and his actor's mind sensed their tremendous dramatic possibilities. The characters, the stories and the scenes seemed to him to cry out for the stage; in fact, he heard that already they were being dramatized.

He was deep in the reading of *Dombey and Son* when he learned that it was in current production back in New York. Here was his character; this Captain Cuttle was made for him. The next day he went into San Francisco to see Tom Maguire. Tom realized that Uncle Billy knew a good thing when he saw it. The play was contracted for by telegraph, the script was mailed, and the play put into rehearsal the next week. Maguire did his usual good work in publicizing the event. Immense posters were displayed about the town with the names of Uncle Billy and Caroline in large type.

Once before their success had been prodigious in a profusion of offerings at the Jenny Lind and the American, and now again the combination was a success. But after two months it was seen that Uncle Billy could not stand the strain. Captain Cuttle was a long, hard part. The Coast production of *Dombey and Son* had to be closed. Uncle Billy's Captain Cuttle was so good that he could not be replaced.

He made a few later appearances but it was evident that his day had passed. At length even Uncle Billy acknowledged it.

Already the city was a far cry from what it had been when William first came to it. After the gold rush came the even greater silver bonanza. The railroad came in. Later there would be oil, wheat and wool.

Uncle Billy, his day drawing to a close, went up to his place at Napa and the family gathered about him. It was a pleasant life for a fellow who could now afford to rest after so many active years. Back of the stable he could sit in the sun hour after hour; all he needed was his wicker chair with the rockers, his bottle of gin and bitters, and his paper to read or use to shoo away the flies. The family was still busy in the city, but they lived with him and his own dear Caroline was of great comfort.

One day as he was sitting in the evening sun they called him to supper but he did not come. They could see him and his chair just keeping on in a slow, easy movement. After three calls they sent one of George's youngsters for him.

The boy came back and said simply, "Grandad can not come."

A gentle breeze had been blowing and had rocked the little old man to that bourne whence no traveler returns.

And in the *San Francisco Bulletin* the obituary notice read: "The best low comedian who has ever appeared in this state."

And in far-off New York Old Ireland would quote the California press on Uncle Billy: "A most meritorious citizen; as a gentleman, kindly-hearted, urbane, and universally esteemed; an industrious, abstemious and most worthy member of society."

*Chambers Street Theatre, New York*

## Chapter *16*

# The Pity of It

Joseph Ireland was by far the best of the contemporary historians of the New York theater during the Chapman period. He was a man who had his favorites, but with small praise even for them. He makes no mention of a Miss Greenwood—Caroline Chapman's early pseudonym. He had probably not heard the gossip about her; that was a secret religiously kept by the professionals.

We have already read his opinion of Harry and Uncle Billy Chapman. That was good enough; but here is what he wrote of Caroline Chapman:

This young lady (not so young that she need to have been unknown to our stage) displayed a meritorious versatility almost unprecedented, and in many characters of low life in comedy was not only unsurpassed but nearly unrivaled. In comic singing parts she was not inferior to Mrs. Fitzwilliams; in burlesque extravaganza she combined the rare merits of Mrs. Vernon with Mrs. Hunt's utter charm; while in the rendering of mock Italian bravura she eclipsed all who have ventured to undertake this experience. Her general style was perfectly original and her chambermaids and rustics were totally free from stage conventionality, yet her points told with greatest force, and in characters like Celeste's French Spy she played with so much dramatic effect that she invariably brought down the house in thunders of applause.

Miss Chapman was slender in person and her features were pleasant if irregular, but her large mouth was redeemed by the whitest of ivory and her whole countenance was radiant with expression from a pair of lustrous dark eyes which could convey at a glance more meaning, either of mirth or sadness, than any contemporaneous female optics of the New York stage.

If Mr. Ireland could have seen Caroline in her *really* great days of Shakespearean playing in San Francisco, he would have held an even higher opinion of her ability.

The name of W. E. Burton is all but forgotten in the annals of the American theater, but for a decade he was the peer of all the stage personalities of the country. He was the editor and a constant contributor to *The Gentleman's Magazine*, one of the leading periodicals of the day, and he had many a lively set-to with Edgar Allan Poe, whose racy style as an associate editor passed before the supervising eye of the actor-manager. Poe, whose mother was an actress, had only contempt for the busi-

ness end of the theater and called Burton a *bill-sticker*.
Burton was much more than a bill-sticker. He managed
theaters in New York and Philadelphia, and wrote for
and played in them at the same time. Almost every leading actor of the day played for him at one time or another. On the programs of the many plays he wrote and
produced can be found the names of Joseph Jefferson,
William Rufus Blake, Henry Placide, Oliver Raymond,
Lysander Thompson, Charles Burke, John Brougham,
Lester Wallack and many a leading actress of the day.
In the writing of a most astute theatrical critic of the
time: "Caroline Chapman was always the heart and life-
blood of the Burton corps." One of Burton's axioms
was, "I keep myself surrounded by talent. No matter
what the cost, it's the cheapest thing you can buy."

Burton's theater was finally assured a success by a
burlesque performance of *Lucia di Lammermoor* in which
Caroline played the lead and sang the original music. It
ran a long time; Miss Chapman was acclaimed the foremost soubrette on the American stage. But it was her
versatility that dazzled critics and audiences alike, for
in comedy she was as fine as Burton himself, and she
was also tenderly appearing in pathetic roles, and up-
roariously funny in farce.

In Doctor Odell's monumental work, *Annals of the
New York Stage*, for the time of Caroline's playing in
the Metropolis, there runs a line of admiration for the
one he never saw:

How I would like to have seen that woman act. . . .
The irresistible comic Caroline Chapman inseparably connected with the memory of Burton's theater in its best

estate . . . the famed Caroline Chapman of Burton's . . .
the delectable Caroline of Burton's . . . one of the most
vivacious soubrettes known to our stage. I must say that
there are few players of the past I should more gladly
have seen than Caroline Chapman. Caroline Chapman
with her humor and ability at parodying the bravura song-
stresses of the day made an immense hit as Lucia in *Lucia
did Sham Amour*, a piece that was seldom absent from
the bills for months thereafter. Lucia was a perfect joy
. . . something like a tear I drop for the departure of
Caroline from Burton's . . . the loss was serious if not
irreparable.

Caroline, until the time of the Chapman exodus to the
West, played child bits, and teen-age misses in New
York and Philadelphia. Life then had seemed natural
enough, but when she was twelve she began to realize
that those of the theater outside her immediate family
seemed to have a strange pity for her. Sensitive to the
feelings of others, she had to be told the truth. This was
not easily done and no choice of words could alter the
fact that she was not, as she had supposed, the daughter
of William Chapman, Sr. She was the child of his son,
Will, and there had been no marriage to her mother, now
long since dead.

The effect of this revelation was profound. Caroline,
with a strong inborn sense of morals and religious lean-
ings, carried the scar of this wound through the rest of
her life. People who later admired her extraordinary
talents on the stage often wondered why her gay laughter and elfinlike quality on the boards faded into such
gravity of manner when the curtain fell.

Efforts were made to disguise the secret of her birth
during her early appearances in New York, and she took

the name of a line of cousins, the Greenwoods. But, with the family a distinct New York success and thus the subject of much talk, the secret could not remain hidden.

A tragic crisis in her life moved her to take again the surname of Chapman, one that is set down in honor in the history of the American Theater. Caroline and Will, united, felt the strong and insoluble bond between them. Will would have owned her, but the sensitive nature of the girl shrank from the disgrace of her origin. They therefore went through life with the public thinking them brother and sister. Their natures worked upon one another and made them both great figures in the world of the stage.

But at the age of sixteen the natural gifts Caroline was later to perfect were secondary in her life. Her reading, beyond the pages of a play, was confined to religious tracts, and all her free time spent in work at an orphan asylum in distant Flatbush. Thus it happened that a young blueblood from Boston, seeing with what great understanding she handled the children in her care, forthwith thought her the one for him to partner and so proceeded toward that end. Caroline, in her secret heart, grew to love him dearly and for a while that love overshadowed all factors that were first, to disconcert, next disrupt, and finally seal the issue.

It was not until sometime after meeting her that he learned she was an actress. This truth was a severe wrench to his New England conscience. He had never been to a theater, but now he felt compelled to attend. It was a rash action of which his Puritan-bound parents would never approve.

Unfortunately, the part he saw Caroline play was the

country wench in *The Way of the World*. His upbring-
ing could not countenance this and he avoided speaking
to her for several days afterward. When he recovered
from that he then had to be told the secret of her birth.
Either shock he may have been able to withstand and
reconcile his parents to, but not both alien facts together.
Within a week he was back in Boston trying to forget.
The forgetting was not easy. In fact, the torment was so
great that he made three trips to New York in search
of her. But by this time Caroline was "Our Caroline" of
the theater in San Francisco, three thousand miles away.

With their experience in the Summer Fair towns in
England and their nine years on the showboat, the
Chapmans could play the gold mines with any kind of
entertainment the rough and ready audiences asked for.
They could sing and dance and tell jokes. They had
scores of comedy acts at their tongue tips. Cold, snow or
rain could not hinder them. They made the dates by
coach, by wagon, on horse or mule back. Theaters could
be made of boards and canvas. They could play in barns,
in the dining rooms of inns or in the open air. Bandits
could infest the roads but the Chapmans had experience
there. The take at the door was not of vital importance.
The miners threw their coins, their watches, their
pouches of nuggets and gold dust on the stage. At times
companies of a thousand strong escorted them from town
to town. So with their pockets lined they went back to
the city to play Sheridan or Shakespeare or anything that
was asked of them.

The Chapmans, until they installed a steam engine on
their craft, floated downstream to New Orleans, took

to horseback and made their return by the *Wilderness Trail.* It took much time, so during the decade on the showboat and the years on the Gold Coast there were lost months in the Chapman saga, months during which they could not be reached nor their exact whereabouts known.

Caroline was the pet of the showboat audiences, which was only an additional inkling of the stellar successes yet to come. In all the history of the theater there probably was never a talent of so wide a range and one wonders at the perfection of all she did. Her mediums of expression were prodigious, not only for the times, but ever since. She played in all of Shakespeare's works, and in many of the contemporary Elizabethan works, all the Restoration comedies, and all the minor dramas of her day. Following her journey to California, and except for once much later in life when she returned to New York for engagements in the East, her stamp is on the Golden Age of the theater in San Francisco.

Young Ed Booth was a member of the Chapman company in the days of barnstorming the camp towns in the gold fields. When he left San Francisco for Australia he was a polished actor with a repertoire of all his father's roles. Junius Brutus, the father, was an actor who rehearsed for himself, careless and indifferent as to what went on behind the footlights. His main concern was that the stage be for his own particular efforts and effects. Naturally, some part of this carried over in the early career of his son Ed, and the critics were not unanimously in praise of his performances, even in *Hamlet;* but to quote the *Alta California* of April 26, 1853:

243

Playing with Ed Booth, Miss Chapman's Ophelia, of course, was excellent, as is everything which this most talented woman undertakes.

In the years of her theatrical activity her "press" was consistently superior. And this despite the fact none of the Chapmans ever engaged a manager or a press agent. They were against puffing and took small delight in seeing their names in the papers.

From the San Francisco *Herald* of June 15, 1853, we again read of Caroline playing Ophelia to the Hamlet of Ed Booth:

> Her representation of the beautiful confiding and unfortunate lady was so effectively rendered, so true to nature as to draw tears to the eyes of her audience. The versatility of this admirable actress is astonishing. In tragedy, in comedy, in melodrama and burlesque she appears equally at home and in all *natural*, piquant and attractive.

And again from the *Alta California*, December 7 of the same year:

> It is no disparagement to any other actress to say that in her particular role of characters she has never had an equal. Of her merits there is, so far as we know, but one opinion and all pronounce her excellent. Of others there is a variety of opinion, but of Miss Chapman nothing is said but in the way of approbation.

The *others* mentioned above were Mrs. Kirby, Madame Sinclair, Matilda Heron and Laura Keen. N. M. Ludlow, of whom mention has been made before, was a man who knew them all. His opinion, then, is of special weight, but finding all the superlatives used up, all he could do for Caroline was echo what everyone already agreed was a fact: "One of the most useful and versatile as is seldom met with. Good in all characters and in certain ones could not be equalled by any actress of the day."

Caroline left behind a small religious booklet on the flyleaf of which is written her opinion of how an actor's work should be publicized.

"There should be no 'puffing,' " she states. "The word of mouth should be the sole measure of an actor's success. What happens upon the stage should be the only magnet to bring people into the theater."

This attitude most probably disguised the worth of this remarkable family. They have been set down by writers since their time as gypsies, small-time actors, the players of minor dramas. They never went out of their way to make friends with the Dunlaps or the Irelands. The truth is that as top artists they antedated the Jeffersons and the Booths and were better trained in the classics of the English theater. From what Caroline did at Burtons on Chambers Street, New York, and at the Jenny Lind in San Francisco, she can be set down here as one of the finest actresses this country ever produced.

But Caroline's life had one more act in its personal drama that harked back through a number of years, a flashback as it were.

After eight years on the West Coast one of the rare miracle men of the theater called her back to New York. His name was Dion Boucicault and among his many talents was the faculty of judging the on-stage value of actors and actresses. This was the man who, with the New York theater thriving and replete with able actresses, sent for Caroline three thousand miles away to appear as Lady Gay Spanker in the revival of his first and most lasting success.

In 1841, when a starving young actor of twenty years, he wrote a play and sent it to the management of Covent Garden. It was in the great day of Charles Mathews and his wife Madame Vestris, one of the most successful combinations ever to grace the London stage.

This was the first wonder. The company paid him three hundred pounds and put the play into rehearsal almost immediately. It was an electric success. *London Assurance* was written with spice and a vital character in a horsey female, Lady Gay Spanker—a part played originally by the beauteous Louise Nesbitt—and one of her speeches became a test for years in judging the quality of the leading ladies of the stage. It was a spirited description of a fox hunt. It could be pointed out that there was no single decent person in the play, but they were stage characters and they dealt in action and with not too many words.

From then on Boucicault was an actor and playwright of enormous achievement. It is estimated that he wrote four hundred plays. It is on record that he had one hundred and twenty-five produced, twenty of them large money-making successes. He fed the theaters of London and New York for fifty years and the total intake of his plays ran into many millions of dollars and pounds.

Many of them were direct steals from old printed pieces of the French theater. He would simply change the locale of the scenes and the names of the characters and smooth out everything at rehearsals; with this method no type of play was beyond his reach. They could be on high society, a rebellion in India, the days of slavery in our deep South, the Yankee life in his time or the peasant life in Ireland. He is the author of the axiom: "Plays are not written. They are rewritten."

He could be original and his greatest successes were his Irish plays, the best part of which were of his own invention. They were all character drawing, situation and action from which the motion picture writers and directors still draw. Every one of his young Irish heroes was sure "a broth of a boy." His character Shaun could outwit and out-talk the bench of the British Court of Law or the Constabulary at any turn. When he stood before the bar and the Judge would ask "Guilty or Not Guilty," Shaun had a ready answer: "Sure that's for you to find out."

There was always moving melodrama, love scenes and comedy in his plays. It's a way with the Irish; he had no illusions about the literary value of many of his pot-boilers. "A degrading occupation," he writes. "I can spin these rough and tumble dramas as a hen lays eggs."

Imbedded in the masonry of the fireplace of his home in Baltimore, William Ferguson, one of the best character actors of Boucicault's time, one could read in large Gothic letters: "Apeing the rich keeps actors poor." It was a quotation from one of Boucicault's plays and the poor man could have profited much in heeding his own warning. He was a hard taskmaster, unpopular in his profession. His career ended in almost dire poverty. In his last days a few of his friends got together and set him up in New York as head of a school of acting. Even that was a failure. He could direct experienced and talented artists of his own choosing. He had no patience with beginners. "The jig is over," he wrote a friend two weeks before he died.

There were very few friends at his funeral and no stone marks his resting place.

He was responsible for Joseph Jefferson's great success in *Rip Van Winkle*. Sam Chapman had dramatized and enacted Irving's story at the Walnut Street Theatre as early as 1828. It had some success, derived mainly from the popularity of the book. But Boucicault's version started Rip as a younger man and it did the trick. Jefferson played it for twenty years.

Caroline's performance had pleased him and plans were made for a production of *Lucia* and other of her former Chambers Street Theatre successes. New York had not forgotten, but ill health beset her. During this stay in New York there was an alarming loss in weight and she hurried back to California. There she began to tire in leading roles before the performance was half over. There soon came a time when she could appear in small parts only, and then in nothing but benefits weeks or months apart. Uncle Billy had returned to California with her. They were never separated in their long professional careers.

Beginning with the year 1860, the fever for the theater in San Francisco began to abate. The gold rush was over. The tragedy of the great war on the Atlantic coast held the national stage. The seas were not free. Emigration stood still. Hard times had come again. There was no money for high-class theatrical productions, and very little money with which to buy tickets for what was produced. There were but small opportunities for an ar-

tist like Caroline Chapman. There were benefits and she
was ready for and active in them all. No matter what the
part she would agree to play it. Her name still had drawing power.

And there was still her love for children. She found
a place for her love in a newly opened orphan asylum
on Bush Street. Almost every morning at eight she reported in and never left before six.

It was here that *he* found her. At first she did not
recognize this strange-looking bearded man in sailor's
jacket and hat.

He spoke her name.

"Caroline. . . ."

She started.

He spoke again. "Caroline—don't you know me, dear?
I remember you. I could never forget you."

"Yes," she said slowly. "I do remember you. But it's
been so long. How did you know where to find me?"

"I've looked all over for you, Caroline. For years I've
searched. That is, whenever I have been in the States.
Today I saw your picture at the desk of a rooming house.
Then it was easy. Everyone in the city knows 'Our Caroline.' The answer to the first person I questioned told
me to come here."

She looked at him intently now. "What are you doing
here?" she asked. "And your family?"

"I cut loose from them forever," he said. "I was dis-
inherited, finally, for spending my time in pursuits other
than adding up figures in a ledger. It was impossible for
me to go back to the old life once I saw it all in true
light. It was hard at first, the seeing, the understanding
—but I don't need them now. Caroline, I'll be rich in

my own right before this war is over. I'll be rich in
another two months. I'll be rich the day I reach New
Orleans. Then I'll come back here and we'll sail ahead
right from where we were tied up."

They had been walking west and were now atop Telegraph Hill.

"What are you doing here?" she asked again.

"I'm the owner of the best brig afloat," he answered.
"It took me years of hard work, but there were wonderful times, too. I've sailed all the seven seas. I've seen all
the great cities of Europe, Asia, Africa, South America.
And all the strange, wild countries—I've seen them too."

"There have been wonderful times for me, too," she
said. "I've lived a good and useful life, I think. But," she
said, contrasting herself to his still youthful and handsome appearance, "a woman wears less easily. Look at me.
My work has had its reward, but it's been hard. I'm going
into the sere and yellow leaf, as we say in the theater. I
never could be now what I once could have been to you.
It's been hard work for me, hard work for the mind and
the body. I'm old, too old for anything but what you
could have seen me doing at that house where you found
me—helping with poor little waifs. While you sailed the
seven seas I have finished my life work and grown quite
old."

"To me, you'll always be just as you were when I
first saw you. You'll always be *Juliet* to me," said the
man of the sea. He pointed. "There she is. Look."

"Where?" asked Caroline. "What is it?"

"There. Right next to the lugger. Can't you pick her
out? She's the finest thing afloat. Just painted. Take
these." He handed her a small spyglass from within his

coat. "Now. Sight right down there to the foot of Market Street. She's the white one," he said. "Can you read what's painted on her prow?"

Caroline could indeed make out the name painted black on white: CAROLINE CHAPMAN.

"I'll have her ready in four days," said the skipper. "Where can I find you of evenings while I'm still in port?"

"Right where you found me today, and at the same time. I take the coach here. It is far to my home, and we are so crowded at the house that I can not take you there without letting them know in advance."

"I'll meet you back there and part with you here," he said. "That's all anyone need know for now. There will be no more interference from families."

"There never was interference from my family," she said, and paused. "I do not know how long you expect to live, but all time is short in this life. I advise you to make peace with your people. Good-bye for now. Here is the coach."

"Now that I've found you," he replied, "that seems a straight and sensible thing to do. I will steer my course by you. Good night."

She smiled and waved to him in an easy graceful gesture as the coach drew away. He stood and looked until it was out of sight.

The next four evenings were as wonderful as he had declared they would be. She still protested about her waning life, but he would not listen. To him she grew more lovely each time they met, and even the people at home noticed that some of her beautiful old spirit seemed coming back to her.

The fourth night came and they stood on Telegraph Hill again. For a half hour they had nothing to say as they looked at the beautiful boat down at the water's edge.

Finally he said, "Take this." He handed her his spyglass. "It's a little beauty. I bought it in Germany. Tomorrow morning, when you leave the coach here right before nine o'clock, watch your ship set sail." He kissed her hand and patted her on the shoulder as she turned away. "Don't look back," he said. "I won't either."

At nine the next morning Caroline stood on the hill and sighted her glass on the boat. She saw the beautiful vessel leave its moorings. She saw the white sails rise and fill. She saw it flow smooth and true through the Golden Gate. She watched it disappear on the horizon. When it was gone she could hardly realize that she had stood there for nearly two hours.

The next morning the blow fell. The first Caroline knew of it was when she heard newsboys yelling it out on the streets: The Confederate gun-running brig *Caroline Chapman* had been captured by a Union gunboat. The ship had been brought back to port with the crew in chains and the thirty-two men were to be held incognito and sent to the Navy Yard in Brooklyn at once. A long jail sentence was the best they could hope for. Caroline never saw or heard from the love of her life again.

Throughout life Caroline's calling was twofold, and following the death of Will she rapidly returned to the attitudes of her early years. So it was until the late seventies that a little old lady dressed in habiliments resembling those of a nun could be seen sprightly walking through the streets of San Francisco on the way to an orphanage or the home of a sick child. Forgotten by her old admirers and unnoticed by the newcomers, she ended her days as she had begun, in deeds of kindness.

*Performance on tree stump, California*

*Chapter 17*

# The Last of the Strollers

George was the first of his generation of Chapmans to reach California, and the last to leave. He outlived Caroline by a few months. His wife saw all but three of her twenty-one children die before her time.

He acted just enough in New York and San Francisco to show that he could do it if he so wanted, but almost all of his many years in California were spent trekking up and down the Pacific Coast from Victoria to Los Angeles with his family, and playing in theaters wherever there were any and, if not, in hotel dining rooms, barns, tents or on the stumps of the massive redwood trees.

He played everything from Hamlet to his own dramatization of *The Fall of the Alamo, or The Death of David Crockett*. He could die on stage in prolonged agony. Once, while with his last few breaths he moaned, "Can this be death?" a voice from the rear of the hall answered, "No it ain't. Get up and sock him." Just how he managed the storming of the Alamo is a mystery.

He was known in San Francisco as a good citizen and fine gentleman, and all of the newspapers ran articles of praise at his death. A tradition in tall tales and humorous stage incidents had grown and multiplied about him. He had his own active sense of humor, too. Like Falstaff he could say: "I am not only witty in myself but the cause that wit is in other men."

He didn't have much success in essaying heavy seriousness, especially on his father's showboat. Still, in that company where everyone acted everything there were times when even he had opportunity to play Hamlet.

One night he was getting through this great role in fine shape. All went well until the graveyard scene. At rehearsal that afternoon George had jumped into Ophelia's grave and bravely defied Laertes; but that night, with another river town date to be made the next day, the steam was up and the floor of the "grave" was the top of the active boiler. The furnace under the boiler was fed with pine knots and tar which could, and did, give forth a heat not unlike the fires of Hades. So George had no sooner jumped into the grave to bid them make Ossa look like a wart than he had to begin a sort of buck and wing dance to ease his burning feet. He climbed out of there before the grave business was completely finished.

And there was a second time when the succulent cat-fish, the unclaimed herald of the Chapman coat of arms, spoiled another perfectly good scene.

During this performance old Chapman had a scene wherein he had to call his servant Francis, played by George. The period of the play was French seventeenth century, and this time there was unexpected modern deviation from the lines as originally written.

At the appropriate place in the play's progress old Will called:

"Francis! Francis!"

There was no answer.

"Francis! Francis!" he called again.

There still was no answer.

Covent Garden Will walked up and down the stage ad-libbing on the weather and whatever else came into his head during the perplexing and unaccountable delay. The play just could not go on until the servant appeared.

Finally, when the delay was becoming apparent to even the audience, George ran on the stage.

"Did you not hear me call?" said Will, getting back to the original lines of the scene.

"Yes, sir," replied the *servant*, thinking to keep in character.

"Then why did'st thou not come?"

This was still off the cue, but there was an answer.

"Because," said George, "I was just hauling in the biggest damn' catfish you ever saw!"

As in the case of all companies, novices were always being added to the cast to fill the minor parts. The production of *The Winter's Tale* necessitated a larger cast than the members of the Chapman clan could muster. A rookie had to be enlisted to fill the part of a bear.

Those familiar with the drama know that the situation demands Antigonus leave the infant Perdita in a remote and desert place where chance may nurse or end it. Then he must get out of the scene and out of the play. The master dramatist does this by having him chased from the stage by a bear. Later it is told how he is killed by the bear, and the ship from which he has just landed wrecked and all lost by a sudden storm. None of the party must get back alive to Sicily, for the babe must be irretrievably lost. A little suspense can be added to the scene by having the bear stop to sniff the babe before continuing the chase.

There are lines to indicate that a storm is brewing, and that is exactly what was going on around the Showboat during the performance. Just as the bear was taking the directed sniff at the babe there was a terrific clap of real thunder. The novice playing the bear happened to be a devout member of the Mother Church, so at the roar from the skies, he stopped to bless himself with the sign of the Cross before he continued the chase.

Improvisation was as much a requirement of the actor as was his ability to read his lines, and a brilliant trick of the time was to use a horse on the stage. In the year 1950 one of the top musical comedy efforts of the New York theater still thought it a novelty to bring George Washington on stage astride a beautiful white charger.

The Chapmans used the idea originally in the tried and true locale of *Sherwood Forest*, with George as the lightning-mettled Robin Hood.

The horse was used in an escape scene. Robin Hood

was being tried before the Sheriff of Nottingham. Asked to testify as to how he had made his escape following a former capture, George's speech in reply was what actors call a "fat one." He described many hairbreadth slips in his victorious gymnastic brushes with the guards of the castle, ending with the line, " . . . Then I run like this."

The only exit from the Sheriff's *court* was by a double center door and the horse was placed just outside, presumably in the *courtyard*, with his head directed off stage. At the end of his speech, George intended to emphasize his last line by a deft sprint and a spring to the animal's back. Then he was to gallop away from the law with all the courtroom in chase through the door. This action, plus the shouts and alarms attending, was the end of the scene and the curtain descended.

A small difficulty presented itself when the horse was first borrowed, brought aboard the showboat and on the stage for rehearsal. The animal was a full fifteen hands high and George spent the best part of two days practicing his leap. Sometimes he bounced from the side of the steed; sometimes he went over the top and fell to the other side. Even when he made a perfect jump the animal seemed reluctant to do his part, that of making away with the escaping Robin Hood.

George sought to overcome this difficulty with two off-stage assistants. He stationed a boy out of sight of the audience with a secondary bridle. The boy was to pull when the vital moment came, and another youngster, behind the horse's haunches and also out of sight, was armed with a wooden slat with which to give the steed a resounding whack. Both of these things were to happen at just the moment Robin Hood was safely seated.

Came the performance, the trials and adventures of Robin Hood all went well for a time. The Sheriff of Nottingham bid him explain his former exploits and George put all he had into the speech, right down to the tag line, ". . . Then I run like this."

He ran like a deer, made a leap like a wildcat and he made it. The boy to the rear swung his slat with all his might.

But the horse was not a real actor. Or maybe he was afflicted with stage fright. Either way, instead of going forward he backed up, pulling the boy with the bridle out into full view of the audience for a sidesplitting climax.

In another instance, George added the role of a Sicilian bandit to his many portrayals. He thought up a grand curtain for his final scene. In the plot's development his one faithful follower had, by mistake, lured him into the clutches of the constabulary and since, of course, justice must triumph, the jig was up.

The *business* of the scene was that the soldiers were to enter four from each side and trap the bandit and his servant center stage. The servant, thus aware of his fatal error and full of remorse, was to fall on his knees before his master, who in turn was to draw his knife and fling it down before the cowering wretch. The weapon was to be so dexterously thrown that it would dig its point into the boards and do a little extra quivering. Then the servant was to take the knife, stab himself to death, and die.

This sacrifice made, George was to dash up the mountain, stage rear. The slope of the mountain was only twenty feet in height, but to the audience sitting below it looked considerably higher and suggested a difficult climb. When George reached the peak he was to turn and give a shout of defiance. The eight soldiers were to raise their guns and, in one mighty blast, *shoot* the Sicilian through and through, giving his portrayer a chance to make a spectacular fall down to stage center for the curtain.

To add realism, George concealed in one of his pockets a sponge saturated with a mixture of beet and walnut juice. This he would clap to his forehead and let the synthetic gore run down his face and white ballet shirt before the thrilling acrobatic stunt of the fall. It would be both tricky and effective.

With the scene in play and the audience all agog, George threw the knife down before his servant. It did not stick or quiver; it broke in two. The handle went one way and the blade another, both out of all reach. This is what actors call a *stopper*, but George was more than equal to the occasion. As one spectator remembered: "He hauled off and gave his cousin Hamilton such a crack in the jaw that he laid dead to all intents and purposes until the scene was over."

Nor was that all. Now was the time for the bloody fall. George dashed up the *mountain* in grand style. He turned and gave a yell of defiance to his would-be captors. The soldiers threw their guns to their shoulders and pulled the triggers. But—the caps were defective and the only sound to issue forth was a few faint clicks audible only to those on the stage. This, when a loud report was all-important, not only to scare the daylights out of the spectators but to be realistic as well, for this was before the invention of the noiseless firearm.

Nevertheless, George clapped his hand to his forehead, the blood came running, and he executed a wonderful fall. The curtain came down to the applause of the audience, who were both thrilled and somewhat puzzled by the whole thing.

One family story of George came from his last visit to the East. He secured an engagement with a touring repertoire company and at once began to strengthen his parts. One little number was a medley he fixed up from the titles of the popular songs of the day. The trick was to combine the tunes and titles to make something that ran along smoothly in somewhat of a senseless story. In California, George had been a far distance from the music publishers of the day, but he studied it through and had it almost ready at the finish of rehearsals. The last line of the medley was "As we were marching through Georgia" and the opening night of the tour happened to be in Richmond, Virginia. So when George finished his song with a full-toned voice and a magnificent gesture, there came from the gallery a multivoiced rebel yell like the magnified scream of a woman. George hurried off the stage and couldn't sleep for three nights.

The elder of the Booth boys, known in the close circle of his friends as Junie, has come down in a story with George Chapman. Junie was an athlete of real fame, one of the best swordsmen of his time and a man of handsome stature, nothing akin to the skinny George. One scheme was known as "take the slap." Its technique consisted in starting a quarrel at a bar and when the argument reached the right pitch Junie was to insert the words "take the slap." At that, the little fellow was to draw back and whiz a fist right past Junie's jaw and within an eighth-inch of it. Junie was to coordinate a hidden hand slap, grasp his face and lower it in a series of groans. When the spectators were sufficiently surprised and excited Junie was to straighten up with a smiling and unmarked face and take a good laugh on everyone.

The last time they played the scene Junie happened to have a newly acquired soldier friend along. When he heard Junie's first moan he hauled off and hit George such a crack that it sent a bothersome loose tooth spinning across the room.

Up in the far North one summer the theater was above the market place and the farmers had stabled some of their livestock that evening to have them ready for the opening in the morning. The play was *Richard III*. After the rising of the curtain the bleating of sheep every now and then harmonized badly with the speeches of the actors. George thought it came from the audience. "My goodness," he said to his wife, "I thought I was a favorite here." He struggled manfully through to the tent scene and at its climax just after he had staggered downstage and shouted, "A horse, a horse, my kingdom for a horse," there came from below him a long, loud neigh of a jackass.

He had reached California in the summer of 1850. There he secured an engagement with one Mr. Barton who had a reputation of never paying a bill or an actor. When artists asked for their stipend his reply was, "Why ask for salaries when berries are ripe?"

Once, an actor with considerable salary due him came to Barton with a sad story of his mother being evicted by the sheriff from the old homestead. The furniture was on the sidewalk, he said.

Barton dug down in his jeans. "You should write her, my boy," he said, "and here's two cents toward a stamp. I'll try to dig up the other penny during the day."

George had heard something of this, but his part in the cast was good and work was work.

So they set out for Sacramento one fair morning in the stagecoach. Before the day was half past the vehicle was held up by a fierce-looking bandit who demanded that their valuables be handed to him through the window. George had visions of another impromptu performance such as that given some years ago in the wilderness.

"Well," said Barton, "this is pretty tough. A man struggles to start a business just to make a living for fellow artists and the first day out he loses his watch." It was an ancient iron-cased article.

The bandit took a closer look from under his mask, handed back the timepiece with a disgusted, "Aw, hell, it's Barton!" turned on his heel and walked off. Evidently he had been an actor himself and knew they had nothing of value.

The little company did not have to live on berries, but there were no salaries. Finally the company had to take over the enterprise to work their way back to the Golden Gate. Barton went his own way.

One local impresario was a cook in a camp. He hired an old shack and put in homemade benches for the audience. It was costing twenty dollars a day to get the company moving and this stand was for two nights. The receipts for the opening were two dollars and ten cents.

George decided to cancel the second show and move on in the morning.

"You're foolish, foolish, foolish, Mr. Chapman," said the cook-turned-manager. "If you stay another night you'll double it."

They finally made it back to San Francisco.

Nothing was heard of Mr. Barton for several years. Then there came a "touch" from him from three hundred miles upstate. All he wanted was enough to get back to O'Farrell Street. George, who had a strong sense of humor off-stage as well as on, sent him a pair of shoes and let it go at that.

One of George's amusement ideas has come down to the present day. It is an outdoor ride patterned on the principle of a whirling upright umbrella with the handle grounded. In the original, the passengers were to take their seats attached to the end of each rib, then the huge protector from rain was to be raised and twirled by means of a hand windlass. Years later one of George's nephews secured a patent on the idea and made a good thing out of it by leasing it out to the county fairs and amusement parks. Its principle is still used.

George was not as lucky with his idea for shooting the apple from the head of his son in the play of *William Tell*.

The apple had already been halved and only needed a touch to have it fall in two clean-cut pieces to the ground. But on the first public try the arrow never found its mark. It ran along a wire and stuck halfway across the stage. The reaction of the audience, accustomed to the accurate bow work of the American Indian, forbade another try.

But George could be something more than a funny man off and on stage.

He could be brave and quick thinking when danger threatened. One afternoon at rehearsal in Sacramento word came that the hospital was afire. George dismissed the rehearsal and rushed his company to the scene. They rescued many of the inmates and the ladies of the company tore their costumes and skirts to make bandages for the injured.

Mrs. Chapman wrote a description of the incident for the *Alta California* in San Francisco, and George and his company were heroic figures in the city and the state.

He passed on in San Francisco in 1876.

*Walnut Street Theatre, Philadelphia*

## Chapter *18*

# The Chapman Sisters

Blanche and Ella, the daughters of Harry Chapman and Julia Drake, came to the notice of John T. Ford when Harry Chapman was John's stage manager at the Holliday Street Theatre in Baltimore. Both girls were talented and Ella was one of the first *Little Eva's*. She was only three or four when she first went to heaven on a wire. She made an attractive heroine, but almost ruined the first night's performance. She forced a ten-minute wait through her tearful backstage insistence that she would not go to heaven unless Uncle Tom was allowed to go with her.

Impressed with their early exhibitions, Ford kept an eye on them after they had moved to New York. They went to school there and played child parts in any theater where their work was requested. There were road engagements as well, but they called Gotham their home. After five years of schooling, their father died. Ford gave them a starring name, *The Chapman Sisters*, and launched them on a brief but most interesting career as a double attraction.

They were a starring team during the years 1864-1868, with Blanche taking a solo lead now and then, and Ella appearing as a singer, dancer and banjo player. Even while playing, the girls took singing, dancing and fencing lessons every day. They were then fourteen and fifteen years of age, Blanche weighing 105, and Ella, 102.

The plays in which they appeared were known as burlesque. It was not burlesque as we know it today, but rather extravaganzas after the manner of the tales in *The Arabian Nights* and the old continental fairy tales. Blanche played the girl, Ella played the boy.

The comedian, and their co-star, was one Charles Bishop; a clever man on the stage. He stood six feet two and weighed over 300 pounds, with a pouch that would do credit to the most corpulent Falstaff that ever fought by the Shrewsbury clock. But for all that, Bishop was sparkling in unction and as light as a kitten on his feet. To see him at work dancing between the two dainty little girls was the highlight of the performance.

Like all comedians, and somewhat like our own George Chapman, Bishop longed to play tragic roles. At last came an offer to play the title role in Shakespeare's *Julius Caesar*. Being basically a good actor, his weight seemed to lend dignity to his early scenes; but when he had been stabbed to death and it was time for the oration over his body, staging difficulties arose. Finally, it was decided that four stalwart men should bring the body of Caesar into the scene on a stretcher.

They had not much more than entered and were crossing the stage to lay the body at Brutus' feet when a loud, vulgar voice from the top gallery sang out, "Holy smoke! He's in the family way!" *Caesar* Bishop arose from his bier, gory wounds and all, advanced to the footlights and made an indignant speech that in no way coincided with the original of the script.

The first tours of the Chapman Sisters were through the South. Poems were written and printed about them in almost every town. The old theater in Savannah was entirely redecorated for them and their likenesses painted much larger than life on the ceiling of the auditorium. Then came the grand tour to the Pacific Coast and a most successful engagement in all the western cities. People had not forgotten their cousins, Caroline Chapman and Julia Dean, and the talent of the two youngsters did them honor. When William Winter wrote his biography of David Belasco, he was requested to include in this handsome edition pictures of the Chapman Sisters, Blanche and Ella.

With the marriage of Blanche and the farewell performance of the Chapman Sisters, Ella took a long step into the amusement world of the day by joining Lydia Thompson and her Blonds. Lydia's company consisted of four British Amazons like herself and a comedian, Willie Edouin. After the first engagement in New York she signed Ella as an ingénue. They played a British burlesque, a lampoon on the lives of the gods on Olympus or on one of the classics of English literature. They sang and danced and told jokes which pleased the audience no end. There was no salaciousness, no double-entendre, no offensive dancing. But Lydia had committed one great fault in the eyes of the Puritans. She had introduced the wearing of tights on the American stage. The effect was electric. The blades, young and old, stood in line to get tickets, and at the stage door to get a closer look at the beauties. From pulpits and news sheets the storm of protest grew and so did the size of the audience. In two seasons Lydia played to a gross of a half million dollars.

One Chicago editor went too far. His paper appeared one morning with the headline: BAWDS IN THE OPERA HOUSE.

The next day Lydia, with one of her Amazons, Pauline Markham, and her manager, Mr. Henderson, met the editor on Wabash Avenue. From beneath her cape Lydia drew a whip and began to belabor the literary gentleman. When her strokes did not seem to have the proper effect, Pauline seized the cowhide and took over, whereupon the editor began to lay about lustily with his cane. This brought Mr. Henderson into the fray with a pistol and he gave the defiler of womanhood several whacks on the head. At this point a policeman appeared and apprehended the whole party. Lydia and Henderson paid fines of one hundred dollars each and the attraction gained nation-wide publicity.

In another town further west the company of Blonds was brought before the Bar of Justice in a crowded courtroom. When the judge had entered and taken his seat he took his revolver from its holster and laid it on the table before him. His first question was to the audience and it squashed the case. "Is there anyone here," he asked, "with anything to say about these ladies?"

The season after the Lydia Thompson tour, Ella made a trip to the Pacific Coast with E. E. Rice's *Evangeline* company. The train stopped off at a siding in the wilds of one of the Western states and she and a number of the company took a walk up the tracks. They sat down for a while on a pile of railroad ties. It started snowing and they had to run back to the train. The next day she discovered that she had lost her purse with her money and some jewels therein. She had no remembrance of where she had lost her wealth. They searched all through the coach and train to no avail.

They played three months on the Coast and then took the train back East. A stop was made at a siding and she took a walk. Of course you've guessed it. The snow was just in the throes of melting and there was her purse on the pile of railroad ties!

But Ella's engagement with the Thompson Company had ended in her becoming very British, and after one more season in America she went to England to become a figure in the great day of the English music hall.

In England those were the good days in the "varieties." Ella could play as many as three music halls a night, driving from one to the other in a privately hired hack. She was well paid abroad, and played as the solo attraction in all the important halls in the British Isles, South Africa and Australia.

Upon her return to London she decided to lengthen and build up her act. To that end she sought to engage

a young man to *feed* her lines in the new skit. She wrote
of her needs to an agent and a young man reported the
next morning. Although he had personal charm, he had
said very few sentences at this first rehearsal before Ella
sensed that it was going to be a task to make a competent
partner of him. Also, her crisp professional manner of
direction made him soon know that she was not to be de-
ceived for long, so he forthwith confessed that he was
not an actor at all. He had been educated as an architect
and was driven to apply for the job by the lack of work
and a sharp case of hunger.

So Ella married him the next week, put all her savings
into the "housing business," as they say in England, and
he became one of the most successful builders of theaters and other public edifices of his time. They had a
difficult siege in the First World War. Her husband had
a stroke and everywhere she moved him, even up as far
as Edinburgh, they were bombed. When he died he left
her a sizable fortune.

Ella was away from America for forty years before
she returned on a visit. She had a hard time finding her
way around in the city she was certain she remembered
well. The elevated railroad had gone up along the lively
Bowery and made a slum of it. Greenwich Village, which
she had known as a quiet residential section, had gone
"arty." The theatrical district had moved uptown. She
recalled having heard a rumor before she first left New
York for England that a Mr. Wallack had an idea he
might build a theater at 31st and Broadway. Everyone
said it would never draw business—not away up there!
But that is where the business had moved to, and a host of
names and faces unknown to her went with it.

There was only one person she could find that she had played with over here. She had first met him on the stage as a singing light opera comedian. Now she found him billed as the country's greatest character tragedian. He was playing Brutus at the Herald Square Theatre. His name was Richard Mansfield. She wrote him a note and he sent her flowers.

She made a point of visiting the resting places of all her dead relatives, before returning to England, and having their headstones brushed up. She even had the bodies in the old Kentucky farm dug up and removed to a proper burial plot in Cincinnati.

Ella also wrote songs. One was a real hit: "He Wanted Something to Play With." The tune was in an English motion picture of very recent date.

Eventually Julia Drake Chapman, her days in the theater at an end, went over from the States to live with Ella. Julia lived to be ninety-four.

Ella lived on to end a beautiful and useful life in 1935. Her last years were ideal. Every day of each month was set aside to entertain some old theatrical friend in her charming little apartment on Kensington. When she passed on she remembered them all in her will with the gift of a handsome jewel from her large and beautiful collection.

Blanche Chapman had been well-trained in the fine points of the stage. Her father, Harry, was the stage manager at the Old Bowery Theatre in New York when all the great ones played there. She had her first speaking part at the age of three and the roles she played as a child with the famous clown, George L. Fox, were long and important.

Fox was a sterling actor as well as a clown and long cherished an ambition to play the weaver in *A Midsummer Night's Dream*. It was at last realized at the Old Bowery, and the morning of the opening the town woke up to find its walls and trees posted with a one-line advertisement: "SEE FOX'S BOTTOM."

A popular actor of the time was one Edward Eddy. He was for the most part all sound and fury, but he had a repertoire that was as extensive as it was varied. The Old Bowery was his favorite house and his engagements there were regular and often. Harry Chapman was of great value to him, not only as a stage director, but as an actor. Eddy boasted that he could give a part a rough study, put it under his pillow at night and wake up letter-perfect in the morning.

Blanche, at that time, was a tall, skinny girl of eleven playing engagements in any New York theater, and even as far off as Brooklyn, when there was a bit part offered. She knew almost every line of the Eddy's Shakespeare repertoire. So, when at eight o'clock one night news came to the theater that the lady who was to play the nurse in *Romeo and Juliet* was taken ill and could not report, they made up and padded the eleven-year-old Blanche, and pushed her out before the audience to play this most difficult role. How well she acquitted herself can be known by the sequel about sixty-five years later.

There was a first-class Shakespeare company playing in Boston, with the story of the ill-starred lovers set for Saturday matinee. Again sickness laid low the lady who was to play the nurse and Blanche was sent for. She arrived Friday afternoon and had one rehearsal. Here is what the reviewers wrote:

A feature of the evening's performance was the appearance of Blanche Chapman, the oldest actress who is still actively engaged behind the footlights, in the part that has taxed the ability of ages of character women. Miss Chapman can read Shakespearean verse in a manner that is seldom heard upon the present-day stage. She learned her art in the days of the great romantic actors, and has at her command a technique that few modern players can equal. Distinction, beauty in delivery, and a rare gift of comedy make her Nurse one of the finest bits of acting that the present season has offered.

In her early training Blanche played one of the apparitions in *Macbeth* with the fabulous Forrest. From the trim athlete of "The Drake Company from Kentucky" days, he had grown into an enormous, obese old man. Still he kept the part of Hamlet in his repertoire. It was distressful to watch. Harry Chapman would not let his children *see* this performance, but bade them sit on the stairs going down to the dressing rooms and listen to the great man *read* the wonderful lines.

Blanche's success was not all in the classical dramatic field; far, far from it. The tours of the Chapman Sisters team were, as we know, a grand sensation. On their Western jaunt they had a unique experience in Virginia City. There lived in this mining capital a young blade formerly of New York. He had been writing his aristocratic mother and sister back East of the great success he was having in the gold fields of Nevada. Gold is where you find it, of course; he was living on the bounty of the owner of the most notorious house of shame in the West.

Two days before the Chapman Sisters were to play the city he received unexpected and, for obvious reasons, devastating news. His mother and sister were on their way to visit him. There was no way to stall them off and no way to extricate himself. He promptly ended his life with a bullet.

Now the sentimental traditions of raw communities was to assert itself. The whole town conspired to announce the death as a natural one and drew the visiting show troupe into the plot. The young man had been something of a poet and the conductor of the touring company was induced to orchestrate one of his works for voice and instrumental accompaniment.

There was a funeral procession past the hotel with a band playing in solemn march the while the Eastern ladies cried on the balcony. That night Blanche sang the song during intermission, with the young man's family in one box and his erstwhile love in the one opposite. The news was broken to the family that the young man had suffered severe losses of late. Four pouches of gold nuggets were all that was left of his fortune, and it went back East with the none-the-wiser ladies from New York.

Blanche could remember the tune and the lyrics of the song to her last days. It went something like this:

> You called me sweet and tender names,
> And gently stroked my golden tresses,
> And swore you'd always be the same,
> And ne'er forget our dear caresses,
> Only last year, only last year
> Only last year in sweet September.

It sounds like a torch song in one of our up-to-date night clubs.

When Blanche married, she did not give up her career. While Ella was reaping success and a fortune in England, the other half of the former sister team was piling up laurels of her own. Her accomplishments stagger the imagination of one of normal ability and energy.

There were many thrills in the long lifetime of Blanche Chapman, but the greatest perhaps was a two-week engagement in Baltimore playing the feminine leads to the exacting repertoire of Edwin Booth. He wanted her to continue, but her family duties forbade it. While taking the calls after the final curtain of the closing night, Booth took the jeweled cross he wore in *Richelieu* and, with a bow, presented it to *Julie de Mortimer*.

It was after that performance that Blanche settled down long enough to raise a family of five. In the meantime the story belongs to Harry Ford, her enterprising husband.

As the first venture of his own, Harry took over the management of the National Theatre in Washington. He prospered there and after a time another theater was built for him in what promised to be a better location. But Harry was too hesitant and indecisive, and the theater did not thrive.

A delegation of two hundred Indians came to the city to visit the "Great White Father." Harry's lawyer came to him with the proposition that the prices be hiked to the government for the tickets of the chiefs and the surplus to be split between the two of them. Harry refused the deal on the ground that it was not honest, so the attorney threw the lease of the new theater to another manager, and a man who kept a stove store down the street stepped in and rented the National.

Harry took the tiny Bijou on Tenth Street, but it proved too small to hold the attractions that came down from Ford's theater in Baltimore. The Bijou had to be used mainly for second-class shows and rentals to amateurs.

One rental was a young stage-struck lawyer who wanted to play Richard III. He secured a date, gathered a company about him and ran notices in the newspapers that the part would be enacted by a young gentleman of the city who had "never before been seen on the stage."

This was an aged ruse to create interest. Garrick used it when first coming into London, but in his case it was not entirely true; he was already a finished actor when he made his London bid. The scheme was probably thought up by a wily press agent he employed. The press agent eventually became well-known as Dr. Samuel Johnson. In this instance the stunt was a huge success: Garrick took the town by storm.

Not so the young Washington attorney. The first scene proved his downfall. As actors put it, "He liked to listen to his own voice," and was going great guns in the murder scene wherein the hunchback *does in* the king. Throughout the speech the voice sank lower and lower.

What, will the aspiring blood of Lancaster
Sink in the ground? I thought it would have mounted.
See how my sword weeps for the poor king's death!
O, may such purple tears be always shed
From those that wish the downfall of our house!
If any spark of life be yet remaining,
Down, down to hell; and say I sent you thither;
I, that have neither pity, lover nor fear.

Right here *Richard* had reason to make a nimble dodging movement, and, advancing to the footlights with fist upraised to the gallery, roared out: "I can lick the so-and-so that threw that egg!"

In another amateur offering there was a quiet love scene where the line "Like the sound of the hunter's horn far distant" was to be spoken. It was thought to be a great invention of stage direction to have the line followed by the true sound coming from afar; in those days it was the custom to have all such effects issue directly from the orchestra pit. Sometimes not only the scenes each had their own special musical theme, but each character had bars for his exits and entrances.

The night of this particular performance the trumpet player failed to show up. The trombonist volunteered to substitute. It was mentioned that it would not quite be the replica of a hunter's horn, but the old gentleman insisted that he could mute his instrument to produce a perfect effect.

The love scene ran along quite smoothly and the hero came easily to the line, "Like the sound of the hunter's horn far distant." Now was the time for the stage effect. But all was quiet. The old trombonist was dozing.

A nudge from a fellow musician aroused him. He grasped his instrument and let out such a blast that it scared the audience half out of their wits, and then kept them laughing for three full minutes.

A general depression came along and the theater business grew steadily worse. Good attractions were hard to find and the lesser ones fared badly at the hands of the critics. One Shakespearean star opened in *Hamlet*. The critics on *The Star* next day gave the performance a column notice without once mentioning the *Prince of Denmark*.

The next night *Othello* was the bill. The notice on that was of more length than had been devoted to the opening. Everything and everybody came in for due notice; with no comment on the title role except that at the end of each paragraph the critic wrote, "But, Oh, Othello." The last paragraph was a sort of résumé of the effort in its entirety and ended—"But, Oh, Oh, Oh, Oh, Othello!"

Harry had to take a pistol from the star to keep him from shooting the editor.

Then one of the stagehands fixing a lamp in the second balcony fell and broke four seats in the orchestra. He was put in the hospital with all bills paid, and the theater disposed of for fear of a damage suit. The man was hospitalized for four weeks. The day of his release he came promptly to the theater, but there was no suit. All he asked for was his hat.

All of these difficulties explain why Blanche came out of retirement. She became a light opera prima donna of note, having seventy-two leading roles at her command. Which meant, in those olden days, that she could walk through the stage door, look at the call board and step out onto the stage and sing any one of those seventy-two parts.

She was the American original in three of the Gilbert and Sullivan operettas and the second *Josephine* in *Pinafore*, at the Chestnut Street Theatre in Philadelphia, in 1878. There was quite a thrill in this presentation. At the opening, Sir Arthur Sullivan himself conducted the orchestra, and this English light opera went on to play an unprecedented one hundred nights.

There were scores of floral decorations sent over the footlights on the closing night. One was a four-masted ship with an anchor of gold inscribed, "To Blanche Chapman Ford, from her sisters, her cousins, and her aunts." She was also always a favorite with the chorus, a respect that is not given without merit.

The next move of the Ford family was to send their daughter, little Ella, for a long visit to her Aunt Ella in England. The boys were sent to boarding school. Harry took a fine actor, Theodore Hamilton, on the road in the dramatization of a new book, *Dr. Jekyll and Mr. Hyde.*

Blanche, in 1882, went on a tour of Mexico with the Hess Opera Company. The cast carried three prima donnas; one for comic opera, one for light opera, and one for grand opera. The climate and the water raised the usual havoc with the cast and put two of these leading ladies to bed. No matter—and almost as lightly as it is told here—Blanche was equal to the task of singing for three.

When the star of George Tyler's *Mrs. Wiggs of the Cabbage Patch* was taken ill and advised by doctors that she should act no longer, Blanche was given the part in New York and put on a train to meet the company, waiting in Omaha. It was a three-day trip. The part was seventy sides. Blanche learned it en route and acted it perfectly the night she joined the company.

This engagement continued for eleven years and then had a long life in stock. Wherever *Mrs. Wiggs* was played by Blanche the play held the all-time record for attendance.

After William Winter had passed on, George Goodall of the *Detroit Free Press* was the dean of American critics. He had a beautifully appointed office, and a handsome bronze bust of Shakespeare stood beside his desk. When Blanche played his city as Mrs. Wiggs he wrote a rapturous notice of her performance. She was intensely proud of the first sentence of his review: "*Blanche Chapman is of the aristocracy of the theatre.*"

But the quality, understanding and gentleness of the lady was by no means limited to the theater. It was in everything she did and in her relations with all people.

It was years later that Blanche performed as the Nurse in the 1927 Boston production of *Romeo and Juliet*. We have already read what one review had to say of that occasion. The following, from the *Boston Herald*, October 12, 1927, merely substantiates what has been said before:

> Juliet's *Nurse* left nothing to be desired. She was priceless throughout. How many Bostonians realized whom they were watching as the nurse? Blanche Chapman has been on the stage for a space of 68 years. She was the original *Iolanthe* and *Princess Ida* in this country. With her acting, the Nurse was presented unforgettably as a lovable, kind old soul who enjoys her power to tantalize Juliet to the fullest, and who is a creature of ice when roused by those who ridicule her but who finally is faithful in her endeavors to bring about the happiness of her adored Juliet.

At the age of seventy-six Blanche took her one fling at "the talkies." She was living in New York then and daily for a week she took the subway to Astoria to appear in a short entitled *Then and Now*.

On the way there the first day she casually remarked, "This may be the turning point of my career."

The little picture went on view as a supplement to the

full-length *Smilin' Through*, which served as a starring vehicle for three outstanding names in the motion picture field of that time. Sime, the sage of Broadway, the founder and an editor of *Variety*, the trade magazine, appointed himself as the one to write the review for his paper. The final sentence of that review is particularly worthy of note: "A character actress of evident long training in 'Then and Now' showed up everyone else when speaking."

Nor was this the end. At the age of eighty-three Blanche studied a sixty-side part in a week and played it in a stock production in Skowhegan, Maine, home of one of the best summer companies in the country. After the first night every seat in the house was sold for the entire week.

Blanche Chapman Ford died at ninety-one—the last of the Chapmans and the Drakes.

*Ford's Theatre, Washington, D.C.*

# Epilogue

The Chapmans and the Booths were companions of the theater for over a hundred years. When Harry Chapman died suddenly, it was thought best that the children should, for the sad months to follow, be taken from the theater and solaced by dear friends. Blanche was sent to the home of Edwin Booth.

Richard Booth, the grandfather of Edwin, was a barrister in London. His forefathers had been driven from Portugal during the Inquisition and came to England by way of Holland. What their name was is hidden in the mists of those early days, but in sound it was probably akin to Booth. After the family had made a name for itself in the theater there was an attempt to trace relationship to a former great English actor, Barton Booth, but that failed in its intention. There were, however, intermarriages with English stock, one with the line of the archradical Wilkes. John Wilkes was a political agitator who stood up in Parliament, called the king a liar, came off unscathed, and went on to become Lord Mayor of London.

This Richard Booth, whose son and grandson we are immediately interested in, was an ardent democrat. He hung a picture of George Washington in the entrance hall of his house and insisted that all callers bow to it. He followed his son, Junius Brutus, to America and fought his legal battles, which was no small assignment. Lucius Junius Brutus Booth started early. He was in trouble with a serving maid while in his teens. At twenty he toured the Low Countries as an actor, making there what his American descendants called a mésalliance. Whatever it was, it rose up to plague him all through his later professional years. A Chapman was stage manager of this troupe.

Back in London from his Continental tour, Booth quickly became one of the city's favorite tragedians. His method was similar to that of Edmund Kean, the effect of his acting like "reading Shakespeare by flashes of lightning." It was inevitable that a rivalry should spring up between these two men, both small in stature and dynamic in emotion. This led to a contest which proved to be Booth's undoing.

He was talked into a joint starring engagement with Kean. The play was *Othello*, with Booth as the wily Venetian and Kean as the choleric Blackamoor. What happened is what will always happen in this tragedy when the actors are equally matched in talent. In the scenes of the first half of the play Iago held the stage; in the last half Othello swept all before him. So in the journals and over the tables of the coffee houses next day Kean easily carried the day.

Booth was so chagrined that he broke his contract, went over to the Covent Garden Theatre and, finally, after playing three years without throwing off the stigma of his defeat, took a boat for far-off lands. With him went a lovely young thing who had been keeping a flower shop near the theater. In the meantime there was a little matter of a road tour to Liverpool where it was rumored he had killed in a duel Diavolo Antonio, a Portugese slack-wire performer much noticed in that city, both in his public capacity and in private circles. This was doubtless an advertising canard.

Booth imparted to the passengers on "The Two Brothers" that he was applying for a position as a keeper of a lighthouse. He probably had something like that in mind as a safe hideaway where his wife could not reach him. But at times his talk was naught but of the theater. It bespoke a towering ambition. It was not a mere inclination, for on finally reaching America he was a success from the start and never quite so wild a character as has been painted. There was a method in part of his madness.

He settled and raised a family near Baltimore. His legal wife turned up with two sons and had to be handsomely provided for. She was divorced and pensioned, and Junius married the ex-flower girl, who proved to be what he often referred to as "an excellent wench." Of the first

287

marriage, one son stuck to his mother until she died in Baltimore in 1858. The other would have nothing to do with the family squabble and finally vanished into thin air. One report was that he joined the Confederate Army and was killed in the Wilderness. Another was that he changed his name, became a doctor, settled in Boston and raised a family.

In the broadsword fights so popular then, Old Booth could tear a passion to tatters, and chase his opponent off the stage and down the stage door alley. Once he followed the poor man out into the public park. But he never did this when there was a man to stand up to him. He finally dropped this method of advertising when in the final scene of *Richard III*, Richmond threw down his sword, took the hunchback King by the throat, and choking him into insensibility, left him prone on the field of Bosworth in exact accordance with the script.

Booth was one of the finest self-advertising actors to appear in those early days. Coming into a play date a day or two before the opening he always contrived to have himself talked about.

On one occasion he came to Cincinnati by steamboat. While still on the river, but within sight of the dock, he jumped overboard with a yell that he had "a message for Conway." (Conway was a well-known English actor who had committed suicide the year before by jumping into the stormy Atlantic.) Booth was an expert swimmer, so he kept going under and coming up until the Chapmans, their showboat anchored nearby, rowed out and pulled him aboard. There he kept insisting that they observe great care in not rocking the boat!

"You'll have us all drowned," he said. The Chapmans

took it all so casually that it didn't make the papers the next day.

But at another time in Cincinnati he did use the clergy to boost his stock. The passenger pigeon, a fancy breed of large *Columbidas*, was then one of the wonders of the Midwest. The flocks were so large that they frequently hid the sun for an hour at a time. At night the branches of the trees broke down with their weight. Day or night, they could be killed in thousands by sticks, stone or shot, which contributed greatly to their final extermination. They were laid along the pavements in heaps for blocks and sold for a nickel a dozen. They were used to fertilize large fields and fed to the hogs.

Booth, in many respects, was a humane man. At his home in Maryland he never allowed anything, not even a fly or a snake, to be killed. Naturally then, the slaughter of these beautiful birds moved him deeply.

So it happened one night that he sent Chapman for the young minister of one of the leading churches in town. He wanted the minister, he said, to perform a hasty burial service over a friend who had unexpectedly come to a sad end. This service was to be held in Booth's quarters at the hotel.

The "man of God" kept the appointment, appearing at the apartment with Book, if not with bell, where the corpse, covered with bed sheets and with candles lit at its head, lay in peace. The obsequies were duly observed and when the last *amen* was intoned, Booth drew the sheets from the body with his favorite sweeping dramatic gesture and revealed the "body" composed of over a hundred dead pigeons.

We need not ponder over the churchman's reaction.

Suffice to say that he indignantly mentioned it in his sermon the next morning—the day before the tragedian's opening night—and set the whole town talking.

It is quite possible that such acts as these were one of the reasons Booth's publicity was not always good. Still it was publicity, and anything novel that made people talk also made a certain percentage of them come to see him on the stage.

His range of devices was endless, his cultural acquisitions prodigious. When he played the Opera House in New Orleans, appearing with a company performing in French, his speech was much more Parisian than theirs. He had lived in Belgium for almost a year, so this was no wonder, but it seemed so to the natives. He spoke four languages fluently and had a smattering of Hebrew.

It has been the consistent statement of writers on the life of Ed Booth that he was sent on tour with his father to keep the great man watched over in his sprees. This is far from the truth. It was a period of hard drinking and Junius Brutus, of British ancestry, could probably hold his own with the American experts. So could Edwin at a later date.

The next to youngest son, John Wilkes, is on record of having put down two bottles of French wine at a two-hour sitting and without a trace of change in his courtly manner. French wine is what we now call brandy. All actors of that time drank heavily, but nonetheless this great artist had much more pride in his profession than any of his three sons. He chose that his mantle should fall upon the shoulders of Edwin. The boy was sent along on the tours to learn his business. With a young, quick mind he knew the lines of all the great parts long before he had a chance to play them. Any actor can tell that this is a far cry from playing the roles. But it is a powerful aid. His first important appearance was as Tressel in the Cibber version of *Richard III*. His father called him to his dressing room, looked him over and reminded him that he was supposed to have just arrived by horse with a message and the first criticism of the *Professor* was, "Where are your spurs?"

No actor before or since has had such training. When he was seventeen he played Richard III successfully in New York. Even as late as 1854 the critics were not overenthusiastic about his Hamlet. They thought he should have been able to play it much more effectively. When he was eighteen he was featured on the billing of his father's engagements as Laertes and Macduff. When he was twenty he was playing Hamlet and other Shakespearean leads in San Francisco with Caroline taking, as the actors say, the notices from him in feminine roles of quite inferior opportunity. And the two Booth boys were supporting her in the Restoration comedies. This was new to them both and they were not too good at it, but there was no fault to be found with Miss Chapman.

Edwin was the most expertly exploited and publicized actor in theatrical history. Three very clever men had a powerful hand in the course of his career. The first was Ben Baker, who fastened himself onto Booth upon the latter's return from Australia, and the ballyhoo was so great that Booth, a naturally modest man, had to protest. Baker came back East with Booth, with the open claim that he had picked up a piece of quartz in California and would make it breed a mountain of pure gold along the Atlantic. He wound up on the long list of Booth's pensioners.

Booth was then fastened onto by an evil genius by the

name of Stuart, who made a three-ring circus of the actor, made him accept financial responsibilities he was never fitted for, and with a wily Boston "angel," finally drove the actor into bankruptcy.

The third man to move Booth ahead and steer him into a sure-fire channel of success was John T. Ford of Baltimore. The circumstances of this will be told later.

That Booth was the greatest actor of his day is not borne out by his brother and sister professionals of that time. By the old-timers that prize was awarded to one John J. Addams, a man built somewhat along the lines of Forrest, but a down East Yankee with much more refinement. Secure in success, a play was written for him with its heroic lead an Indian chieftain, a popular subject of the time. It was a complete failure. Forrest had a like ambition and followed Addam's effort with *Metomora*. It was a poor play and a great success. From that time Addams' star began to fade. He drank himself to death at age forty-one and died alone and forsaken in a garret in Cincinnati. Booth also had in his best day a leading man in Edward Adams, a product along with Booth and his first wife, Mary Devlin, of the John T. Ford stock company in Richmond, Virginia. Joseph Jefferson was the stage manager of this company.

When the great Booth Theatre on Sixth Avenue in New York was opened, the notices were about the tremendous physical aspects of the house. It was a wonderful achievement for the municipality, but a careful reading of the lines gives one the impression that while Booth had the well-wishers, Adams had the greater talent. The same was true when the company followed *Romeo and Juliet* with *Othello*, with Booth and Adams alternating in the parts of Othello and Iago. Adams finally got his salary with Booth up as high as three hundred dollars a week, an unheard of sum for a supporting actor in that day. He wound up as a road star.

Walt Whitman, a nurse in Washington during the Civil War, an ardent follower of the theater and the most consistent champion pass-grabber of all time, said that Ed Booth "had everything but guts," probably the first use of that now quite common expression; and Ellser, a prominent manager and certainly a fine judge of acting, had the boldness to say that "Wilkes Booth had more of the old man's power in one performance than Edwin can show in a year." In a letter to Winter, Ed lets the cat out of the bag as to what the British reviewers thought of him. He writes: "They say my Iago is 'clever' and my Othello 'feeble!' "

In his London engagement with Henry Irving, Ed Booth was amazed at the care and exactness the English star put into rehearsals. When his father had been asked by a young actor on what would be his position in the scene, the old man, who was unconcerned about exacting details, replied, "I'll find you." The London stage of that time was different. The perfection of scenic and stage business in Shakespearean productions reached its zenith during the time of Charles Kean, Henry Irving and Beerbohm Tree.

In one of Kean's rehearsals he noticed a young actor was listless and not alert to cues. Taken to task, the young actor remarked that it was unnecessary to rehearse him at all because "I know the part backwards." He received a gentle reminder from Kean, "I know you do but that is not the way I play it."

Booth's notices in London were what an actor would call *mixed*. "He thinks the part better than he acts it. . . . He stirs no pulse and leaves the heart unmoved even in the finest passages of the play."

In alternating the parts of Othello and Iago with Irving, one notices how differently these two great actors played Iago. Booth plotted him as a straight villain. Irving played the Venetian as a gay sort of brainy devil smoking a long pipe. It is probable that there was a touch of insular jealousy in the reviews and that both were very effective.

Ed Booth may have lacked power for the style of acting of his time, but there is no doubt that, in what the actors call "giving a reading," he knew all the vocal lights and shades and the practiced art of facial expression and gesticulation. In soliloquies he has never been surpassed. This made his Hamlet great. When someone suggested to Wilkes that he play the part he said, "No, that is for Ned. He is Hamlet, melancholy and all." There were bad moments in his appraisal of his choice of a life work. When a young acquaintance wrote him that he contemplated giving up his business position to throw his lot in with the artists of the stage, Booth replied as follows:

I was indeed startled and, I must confess, pained by your letter announcing your determination to abandon your profession for that of the stage, and in sincere frankness must beg of you to reconsider the matter, for I really have no hope for a satisfactory result from such a change.

The feelings that prompt you to take this step—I mean your "love, enthusiasm and natural inclination"—do not imply an ability for the art. There are hundreds of disappointed lives wasting on the stage when they felt as you do, that a brilliant destiny awaited them.

You may be able to recite in public in perfect ease and propriety, even with the highest excellence, and yet have no other qualification for the highest form of dramatic expression.

Mr. Field of Boston is to be my manager for next season and I have already applied to him for positions, but in vain. I have just sealed a letter to a young and talented lady friend in Paris containing Mr. Field's reply to my appeal in her behalf—the second letter he had sent me in response to favors I have asked for friends—consequently I will return the application you enclosed to me, for I know it is useless to send it to him. He has one of the few regular companies, engaged permanently I mean, in this country and he keeps the best of them "year in and year out" as long as he can.

You can form no idea of the many who solicit my influence every season, professionals and amateurs, friends and strangers of all qualities, male and female. 'Tis very seldom that I can serve them, for managers prefer to judge for themselves and as my "support," no matter how capable it may be, had been abused by the press for many years past and will always be to the end of my career. My recommendation is not respected by managers, whose judgment is greatly influenced by what the critics say.

I have known many, like you, give up home, friends and responsible positions for the glitter of the actor's calling and who are now fixed for life in subordinate positions unworthy of their breeding, education and natural refinement.

I beg you as your friend and sincere well-wisher to abandon this mistaken resolve and enjoy the drama as a spectator with pleasure, something as an actor you would never know, and retain the family friends and happy home that are now yours.

*Had nature fitted me for any other calling I would never have chosen the Stage. Were I able to employ my thought and labor in anything else I would gladly turn my back on the Theater forever.* An art whose professionals and followers should be of the highest culture is the mere make-shift of every speculator and boor that can hire a theater or get hold of some sensational rubbish to gull the public. *I am not very much in love with my calling* as it now is (and as I fear will ever be), therefore you see how loathe I am to encourage anyone to adopt it. I hope you will take my advice as it is meant in sincere kindness, and believe that my only wish is to spare you the sorrow that must follow the course you would pursue.

With cordial regard for yourself and family, I am truly yours,

Edwin Booth.

There is no doubt in the world that he was personally a wonderful man, beloved by all. He maintained a long list of pensioners, he will always remain an inspiration and his establishment of The Players Club and the Actors' Fund of America were acts of rare service. His sorrows in life were hard to bear. His achievements have never been surpassed. His rewards as an actor were magnificent.

John T. Ford of the Baltimore Theatre was one of the few managers for whom Ed Booth had the highest respect. He was the originator of the *all-star cast* in America. From all over the country he brought to Baltimore a one-night performance of *She Stoops to Conquer*. Most of the cast came from the wonderful stock company he had been operating in Richmond, with Ed Booth as the juvenile, Mary Devlin as the ingénue, and Joe Jefferson as stage manager. John T. brought them together and

Harry Chapman directed this performance. There was but one rehearsal on the morning of the play night. Everyone had played their part many times before and knew the lines and most of "the business." The next morning all went back where they came from and the regular stock company went back into the run of *Seven Degrees of Crime*, a prison melodrama written by John T. Ford and staged by Harry Chapman. For the single performance of *She Stoops to Conquer* artists came from New York, Boston, Richmond and Cincinnati.

Ed Booth always remained in the highest form of friendship with John T. Ford, as the following letter testifies:

My dear Ford;

Though rapidly improving in the general state of my health, I have many aches and cramps—my elbow joint is stiff and the entire arm useless. I hope I may be able to resume my work in a fortnight or less. Mary now suffers from the reaction of the great strain upon her nervous system and if she did not have the wonderful will power you speak of she'd be as my larboard fin is—in a sling—but she keeps up like a perfect She-ro (this being the feminine I presume of Hero and Nero, the neuter gender). N'est-ce pas? There's a French lick at you in return for yours. In other words, an Oliver for your Roland.

My wife joins me in kind regards to yourself and all the Fords we know.

Truly yours,<br>Edwin Booth

N.B. This is a "Love Hand" dealt you.

This N.B. seems to be in a lighter hand, which may or may not be Booth's. It may be that of Mary McVicker,

with whom Ford may have expected a little trouble during the conceiving of an idea he had for a Booth tour
through the South. John thought she could not act very
well. In any case, Mary McVicker acted but very few
times after this and the postscript to the letter may be
an indication that all will be forgiven. Mary made much
trouble for Booth's business associates. The poor lady
finally became insane and died.

Booth was often criticized for the caliber of his company. At John's insistence, the cast on the trip through
the South turned out to be one of the best he ever had.
Ford strengthened the local companies where Booth
appeared as a guest star, sent on special actors for special,
particular roles and engaged as many as fifty supernumeraries for the various battle and court scenes of the
plays.

In April, at the end of every season, John T. Ford ran
a two-week Shakespearean revival with Preston Clark,
Booth's nephew, the leading player, and a handsome
present for everyone who bought a ticket for the opening night. Baltimore was not too Stratford-minded at this
time. There was always a severe loss on these engagements. One of the opening-night presents was a small
china pitcher imported from England, with the Bard's
picture on one side and his birthplace on the other. It
now finds its place in the most swank antique shops. In
this, John T. seemed to have been the originator of the
modern motion picture houses' gimmick of giveaway
table china sets piece by piece.

None of Booth's sons had their father's talent for
publicity. When quite young they played a week of
standard tragedies at the old Holliday Street Theatre in

Baltimore. Harry C. Ford, destined to be the husband of
Blanche Chapman, was the boy treasurer. Receipts for
the eight performances amounted to $146.00.

Later, when John T. Ford was one of the most successful theater operators in the country and manager
of the Chapman Sisters, Blanche and Ella, he realized his
inspiration of this starring tour of Edwin Booth as
Hamlet in a tour of the Southern states.

Thus, he had written to Ed Booth asking terms for the
projected Southern tour. Edwin thought it over for a
week and then replied in a lengthy letter. He asked
$500.00 a performance, an unheard-of guarantee in those
days. Very few of the profession thought he was worth
it. Just eight months before he had been cleared from
bankruptcy. He had played one engagement of his favorite roles at Daly's Theatre. All of his friends and well-
wishers thought it another great success, but the press
was not so sure. One reviewer gave it as his clear opinion
that Booth, at the age of forty, had seen his best days.

With this price tag on his services, all of John's associates strongly advised against such a tour. They brought
up the argument that so soon after the War between the
States the South was too poor to pay for such a non-
essential, and the fact that Edwin's brother, John Wilkes,
had killed the President had made conditions more harsh
for the South than they probably would have been other-
wise.

On the other hand there was advice to ease in a mid-
week matinee and offer $3,500 for an eight performance
week. John's telegram in reply was of but one word:
Accept. That was the only written agreement between
the parties of the first and second part.

The tour opened in Baltimore for two weeks, but before the opening it was clearly evident that the leading lady Lilli Glover was not up to playing the leads in the repertoire. Blanche Chapman was enlisted to take her place. With the vast knowledge she had of every play and her professional quick study, she acquitted herself so nobly that Booth, during the calls after the final curtain of *Richelieu*, unclasped a rich stage jewel he wore and presented it to her. He wanted her to continue to tour, but Blanche had a family of three by then and wanted to retire for the time being. The next week there came to her a handsome silver tea and coffee set.

Along the entire tour route, crowds seemed to spring from the ground. The theaters were given for nothing. Booth himself was astonished and a little regretful that he had not asked for more, but he lived strictly up to the one-word contract. It was a turning point in a great career. Ed Booth now knew that there was a fortune for him "on the road" and in the matter of business his brother's death was more of a help than a hindrance.

The company consisted for the most part of artists from Ford's stock companies with Frederick Warde as leading man. He afterward became a noted Shakespearean star. The crowds on the streets became a severe annoyance to Booth. Everyone wanted to see the brother of the man who shot Lincoln. One of the company with a build like a massive Edwin Forrest grew a goatee and was pointed out by the company as Booth. This lessened the strain on the star. A remark by John Moray, an enthusiastic theater-goer, that Ed Booth's great success was due to alternately standing on the tombstones of his father and brother had a small degree of truth.

John Wilkes Booth had been buried in the courtyard of the old Capitol Prison in Washington, but his family could never be satisfied until his remains were removed to the Booth burial ground in Baltimore. John Ford and his brother Harry were urged to gain permission from the Government to make the transfer. Ed Booth would never enter the city of Washington after the tragedy of the Lincoln assassination. Whenever he had occasion to go South he would, from Baltimore, travel out through the Shenandoah Valley so as to avoid the national capital.

The Ford brothers made the request several times and it was finally granted with the admonition that, for obvious reasons, there be not a whisper of publicity. The body was disinterred and taken to an undertaker where it was identified by a dentist and a doctor who had performed a slight operation on Booth's neck.

Harry Ford was there with Blanche, and when she asked if he was certain that it was the body they wanted taken to Baltimore, he replied: "I knew Wilkes Booth better than I know you, and there is no need of doctor or dentist. One look told me that was all that was left of my friend." It was a hard part in life he had to play at that time. He considered Lincoln to be a great, good man and Wilkes Booth to be one of his dear friends. He also thought Mrs. Mary Surratt to be entirely innocent. He thought the principal witness against her was frightened of his own safety and wanting to be a good witness, slanted in his testimony one action and one remark made by Mrs. Surratt. Even if everything he said was true, it was insufficient testimony for a hanging. The worst actual act against the poor lady was that Payne, after wandering and hiding for several days, came to her house

to get what news he could. He got there just as the de-
tectives were leaving the house with her after making
the arrest. She said she did not know him. At best she
knew him only slightly. It was dusk on a dark day, Mrs.
Surratt was definitely nearsighted, and Payne was in
disguise. The Fords arranged for the shipment of the
body and John wired to Ed Booth in Baltimore. "Success," was the one word he used.

Harry would never talk much about the Lincoln
tragedy except to say that Booth was one of the finest
gentlemen he had ever met, which seems to have been
the general opinion of all who knew him. Harry did say
once that he had chided Booth on the company he was
keeping, but all the latter would say was that it was all
part of a plan and would come out right in the end. Sir
Charles Wyndam and Clara Morris have given like testimony. Harry knew all of the conspirators by sight but
none of them to speak to.

Dick Ford went to the White House the morning of
the tragedy. He had never been able to see Mrs. Lincoln,
but he knew that she was the one to reach with an invita-
tion to the White House family to attend a performance.
He could usually get the request to her through one of
the maids whom he knew. He had finished this part of
his task, and on his way out of the White House he met
the President walking alone to one of the offices. He
asked him, "How do you feel, Mr. President?" Lincoln's
reply was characteristic. "Like a boy," he said.

At noon of the day of the assassination, Harry was
standing at the front entrance of the theater conversing
with two friends when he saw Booth approaching. He

came at noon almost every day for his mail. "Here comes the handsomest man in Washington," was a remark Harry made and remembered.

In his few lapses from silence Harry would say that he had never read a book or article on the assassination that was free of mistakes. He was sure that, although it had been mentioned, there was no intent in the mind of Booth to kill the President until the afternoon of the very day it happened. Booth did not know of the intended visit of the President to the theater until early afternoon of the fatal day. There was a year-old plot to kidnap Lincoln, and for that purpose Booth had gathered around him a group of malcontents and Southern sympathizers of the lunatic fringe.

Wilkes' sparkling success had been made, for the most part, in the South. At least, that is where his financial rewards were the greatest. He was making twenty thousand dollars a year. He did not have to quit the theater, as has been written, on account of a loss of his voice. With the drafty theaters, hotels and trains of those days all actors had laryngitis from time to time, but no actor ever quit the stage because he had a sore throat or had lost his voice. It always came back. That he invested money in oil stock does not indicate from what had occurred since that he had a total lack of business acumen. He had leased a theater in Washington, engaged the cast, staged the heavy repertoire and billed himself as *The People's Choice*. His voice was as clear as a bell when he played Anthony to the Brutus of Ed and the Cassius of Junie in the benefit performance of *Julius Caesar* at the Winter Garden for the completion of the fund for the erection of the statue of Shakespeare in

Central Park. This was in November, 1864. Anthony is a hard part to take over with a poor voice. On the curtain calls Wilkes received the greatest applause.

When Wilkes heard from Harry that the President would attend the performance that night, he said something to the effect that "Lee should never have given up his sword." There was something strange in his next action, although it did not seem so to Harry at the time. He took from his wallet a small photograph of himself and gave it to Harry.

"I had only two left," he said, "and I gave one to Bessie." Bessie was one of his sweethearts at the time. She was the daughter of a senator and she later married a senator. She survived her husband and when, after her death, her lawyer examined her papers he found a package of letters from John Wilkes Booth, kept all those years. They were destroyed.

Harry was always quite sure he put the picture in his pocket, but he never knew what became of it. It disappeared with the box office pistol he sometimes carried. Years later the picture and the pistol came back in the mail, anonymously but probably the act of a friendly detective or policeman.

When Wilkes came into the theater that night, Harry was at the ticket window. Booth came over to him and laid the butt of his cigar on the shelf. He then read a parody on a well-known line in the then popular burlesque, "Bombastius Furiuso": "Who 'ere this cigar shall replace, shall meet John Wilkes Booth face to face." He nodded to the ticket taker as he passed into the theater and went up into the gallery to do what he had planned.

Harry later told Blanche it was his thought that Booth

had sent word to his fellow conspirators to meet in the
back room of a saloon on the other side of Pennsylvania
Avenue, and that it was there and at this late hour that
the plan to assassinate was hatched. But not by Booth.
He had been resorting to what they called "French wine"
for the past two years, and in this drugged way had kept
his spirits up. He had drawn scarcely a sober breath for
a full day during that time, but there was always the
thought of a last shout for glory to kidnap Lincoln and
win the admiration of both the North and the South by
the daring of the deed. It is hard at this present day to
realize the propaganda against Lincoln in the South and
the hatred it aroused.

John Surratt probably got a summons to attend the
meeting and sensed that it indicated murder might be
attempted. He jumped town toward Canada that night.
From there he managed to get abroad by taking ship to
Europe, made his way to Rome and enlisted in the Papal
Guards. A few years later some American visitors to
Italy passed him, and Surratt realized that he had been
recognized. He took flight again and was captured in
Egypt. He was brought back to Baltimore and tried, but
the jury was hung and he grew into an old, long-bearded
man working as a clerk for an express company.

Harry's thoughts on the motives of the conspirators
were that, in his quest for assistance, Booth had picked
up one Lewis Payne, a bounty jumper from both armies
and a fearless killer, maddened by the loss of a brother
while by his side at Antietam. Payne was the son of a
Methodist Minister with more than an average schooling.
He was a dark, handsome, six-foot-two athlete of a man
entirely ruined by four years at war. At this last meeting,

with the French wine flowing freely, Payne took charge. He made fun of their kidnap plot as a play-acting dream, unrealistic and impossible to succeed. Now was the time to kill, he told them. It was easier and would be more effective in bringing the South from her knees to a fighting position again. Booth, angered by the taunts, in stagey bravado offered to take Lincoln and have the business done with. He knew where to find him: In a theater where there was an audience. He could act. Payne said he would take Seward, the rest of the cabinet was allotted, and the killing was in order.

The actual story of the murder of Lincoln is well known. Booth and Payne were the only two to go through with the plot. Booth did that with which he had been charged. Payne had less success. He reached Seward on a sickbed and wounded him severely, but was driven off. He was the fearless desperado to the end. On the way to the scaffold he passed a corporal standing a step ahead of his squad. It was a blazing hot day. Payne reached over, took the corporal's hat and put it on his own head. He evidently wanted to be free from sunstroke in the last half hour of his life.

Harry had a room in the house next door to the theater and had a door cut through the wall into the theater balcony to avoid the rainy weather and muddy pavement. The street was a dirt road at the time, with tar torches stuck in barrels nightly, running down to Pennsylvania Avenue, with barkers at each barrel yelling "This way to Ford's." Through this door Harry had carried his chair into the presidential box for Mr. Lincoln's comfort. Years later he heard that the chair was on exhibition in the cellar of the Capitol and he took a trip over to see if they had the authentic article. A guard was giving a small crowd a short lecture on the chair and called attention to the stain of Lincoln's blood. Harry's young son, whom he had brought along, noticed his father smiling as they were walking away at the end of the lecture. The boy asked why.

"When I was a young spark," said his father, "I used bear's grease to polish up my hair. That wasn't Lincoln's blood. That was my hair oil."

**END**

# Index

# Index

311

¶ This book is set in Janson, a distinguished old style face which is presumed to be Dutch in origin. Anton Janson, a Leipsic punch cutter and type founder, issued it sometime during the latter half of the seventeenth century. The Linotype recutting of Janson was made from type cast from the original matrices. ¶ This book was designed by Myrtle Powell and composed, printed and bound by The Haddon Craftsmen.

## DATE DUE

| | | | |
|---|---|---|---|
| | | | |
| | | | |
| | | | |
| | | | |
| | | | |
| | | | |
| | | | |
| | | | |
| | | | |
| | | | |
| | | | |
| | | | |
| | | | |
| | | | |
| | | | |
| | | | |
| GAYLORD | | | PRINTED IN U.S.A. |